Good Housekeeping's
COOKING for COMPANY

By the
Food Editors
of
Good
Housekeeping
Magazine

ILLUSTRATIONS BY
KINUKO CRAFT

PHOTOGRAPHS BY
JAMES VILES

Published by
Consolidated Book Publishers
1727 South Indiana Avenue, Chicago, Illinois 60616

Contents

Simplicity, not convention, should determine the rules if you want a serene but maidless luncheon. Set up a lovely luncheon table (or tables) using an attractive cloth or place mats. Place a 9-inch luncheon plate in center of each place, 1 inch in from edge of table or mat. Fold napkins into oblongs; lay on luncheon plates. (Or if you are serving a first course, place napkin to left of fork.) Set each place with flat silver, 1 inch in from edge of table or mat as in the diagram below. (Add dessert silver when dessert is served.) Also arrange plates, glasses, etc., as shown. To save energy (and dishwashing) you may dispense with bread-and-butter plates. Set a 7- or 8-inch plate to left of napkin to hold both salad and bread. Dispense with salad forks and let guests use luncheon forks for both main course and salad. Dispense with butter spreaders by pre-buttering hot breads. Starred recipes (*) in menus appear below.

Luncheons for 4, 6, 8, and 10

1   9-INCH LUNCHEON PLATE FOR MAIN COURSE
2   7- OR 8-INCH PLATE
3   BREAD-AND-BUTTER PLATE WITH BUTTER SPREADER ACROSS IT
4   LUNCHEON FORK TO BE USED FOR BOTH MAIN COURSE AND SALAD
5   LUNCHEON KNIFE
6   TEASPOON FOR FRUIT COCKTAIL (OR SOUP SPOON)
7   WATER GLASS
8   FRUIT-COCKTAIL GLASS
9   LUNCHEON NAPKIN, FOLDED INTO OBLONG

641.5
G

THREE-LAYER-SALAD LUNCHEON
Shrimp-Parfait Salad* with Ham Roll-Ups
Blue Cheese-Walnut Balls*   *Crisp Crackers*
Spongecake Slices with Melba Sauce   *Coffee*

SHRIMP-PARFAIT SALAD

Carrot-Apple Salad, below   6 tomato slices, quartered
Radish Slaw, below   6 pitted ripe olives
Curry-Shrimp Salad, below   6 cooked ham slices, each rolled up
6 radish roses   Crisp crackers

Early on day, if desired:
Prepare salads, and radish roses. Refrigerate all.
About 30 minutes before serving:
1. In each of 6 tall goblets or glasses, arrange layer of Carrot-Apple Salad, then one of Radish Slaw. Top with quartered tomato slice, then a layer each of Curry-Shrimp Salad and Radish Slaw.
2. Crown each serving with more Curry-Shrimp Salad and Radish Slaw, then an olive and a reserved shrimp *as pictured opposite.*
3. Now, on each of 6 luncheon plates, center one of parfait salads. Around each group a ham roll-up, 3 Blue Cheese-Walnut Balls, a radish rose, and a few crackers. Makes 6 servings.

Carrot-Apple Salad

1½ cups coarsely-grated carrots   1 tablespoon cold water
1 cup coarsely-grated unpared   1 tablespoon granulated sugar
  apples   ¼ teaspoon salt
1 tablespoon lemon juice   Whipped cream

Early on day, if desired:
In bowl combine carrots, apples, lemon juice, water, sugar, salt, and ⅓ cup whipped cream;* cover; refrigerate until served.
*For ⅓ cup whipped cream used in Carrot-Apple Salad and in Curry-Shrimp Salad, whip ⅓ cup heavy cream, then divide.

Radish Slaw

5¼ cups coarsely-grated cabbage   1½ tablespoons light cream
⅓ cup chopped onion   1 tablespoon lemon juice
½ cup chopped celery   ⅛ teaspoon pepper
½ cup chopped green pepper   1½ teaspoons granulated sugar
¾ cup sliced radishes   ¾ teaspoon salt
½ cup mayonnaise

Early on day, if desired:
1. In large bowl combine vegetables.
2. In small bowl combine mayonnaise, cream, lemon juice, pepper, sugar, and salt. Pour over vegetables; toss. Cover; refrigerate.

Curry-Shrimp Salad

1¾ pounds cooked, cleaned shrimp   ⅛ teaspoon salt
⅓ cup mayonnaise   ⅛ teaspoon pepper
⅓ cup whipped cream*   ½ teaspoon granulated sugar
2 teaspoons lemon juice   ¼ teaspoon curry powder

Early on day, if desired:
1. Refrigerate 6 nice shrimp. Cut rest of shrimp in halves or thirds.

Shrimp-Parfait Salad

Melon Change-About

Chilled Lobster Soufflé with Sherry Aspic

2. In bowl combine mayonnaise, whipped cream,* lemon juice, salt, pepper, sugar, and curry powder. Fold in cut-up shrimp. Cover; refrigerate until served. *Leftover from Carrot-Apple Salad.

BLUE CHEESE-WALNUT BALLS

2 5-ounce jars pasteurized blue-cheese spread   ¾ cup chopped walnuts

Early on day:
Shape cheese into 18 balls. Roll in chopped nuts. Refrigerate until served.

LIGHT LUNCHEON FARE
Chilled Lobster Soufflé* with Sherry Aspic*
Hot Parkerhouse Rolls
Melon Change-About*
Coffee

CHILLED LOBSTER SOUFFLÉ

4 or 5 10-ounce packages frozen rock lobster tails (4 cups meat)
3 tablespoons butter or margarine
¼ cup regular all-purpose flour
¼ teaspoon pepper
1 teaspoon salt
Dash paprika
2 cups milk

1 10½-ounce can condensed beef bouillon, undiluted
2 envelopes unflavored gelatin
6 tablespoons sherry
4 egg whites
3 cups heavy cream
Sherry Aspic, below
¼ cup snipped parsley
Lemon wedges (optional)
Lettuce

Day before:
1. Fold a 30-inch length of foil, 12 inches wide, in half lengthwise; wrap around outside of china soufflé dish which measures 7 cups to brim, so that a collar 3 inches high stands above rim; fasten with cellophane tape. Lightly grease inside surface of foil only.
2. Boil lobster tails as package label directs; drain; cool.
3. Meanwhile, prepare white sauce: In medium saucepan, over low heat, melt butter; stir in flour, pepper, salt, and paprika until blended and smooth. Slowly add milk, stirring constantly. Cook, stirring, until smooth and thickened; remove from heat; cool.
4. Now remove lobster meat from shells; then, into 3-quart bowl cut lobster meat in bite-size chunks (reserve 1 cup). Into small saucepan put bouillon; sprinkle on gelatin; stir, over low heat, until gelatin is dissolved. Remove from heat; stir in sherry. Stir into cooled white sauce, then pour over chunks of lobster. Refrigerate until slightly thickened.
5. Beat egg whites until stiff, but not dry. Then beat cream until soft peaks form. Fold egg whites and

whipped cream into lobster mixture. Pour enough into prepared soufflé dish to come up to rim. Top with reserved lobster meat. Pour rest of soufflé over it. Refrigerate at least 6 hours.
6. Meanwhile, prepare Sherry Aspic.
About 15 minutes before serving:
1. Peel off foil collar, using small metal spatula, dipped in water, to help loosen it. Gently press snipped parsley all around sides.
2. With small, sharp knife, cut Sherry Aspic into 40 to 45 tiny cubes. Pile it in center of soufflé. Then, if desired, place lobster claws around aspic cubes *as pictured on page 3.*
3. Garnish with lemon wedges. Let each guest spoon some of soufflé into crisp lettuce cups. Makes 8 to 10 main-dish servings.

SHERRY ASPIC: Into small saucepan empty 1 10½-ounce can condensed beef consommé, undiluted. Sprinkle on 2 teaspoons unflavored gelatin; stir over low heat until gelatin is dissolved. Remove from heat; stir in ¼ cup sherry. Turn into 9-by-5-by-3-inch loaf pan; refrigerate.

MELON CHANGE-ABOUT

1 cantaloupe
1 honeydew melon
½ cup white corn syrup

¼ cup lemon juice
Fresh mint sprigs
Dash mace or nutmeg

Early on day:
1. Halve melons lengthwise; remove seeds. Then cut each half into 4 wedges.
2. With melon baller remove 3 balls from each wedge. Then tuck honeydew balls in cantaloupe, and cantaloupe balls in honeydew *as pictured on page 3.* Refrigerate.
3. Make mint sauce: Stir together corn syrup, lemon juice, 2 tablespoons snipped mint, and mace. Refrigerate.
At serving time:
Arrange cantaloupe alternately with honeydew wedges on platter, spoke-fashion, with a few mint sprigs in center. Serve a wedge of each kind to each guest. Pass mint sauce. Makes 8 servings.

LUNCHEON BY THE POOL
Frozen Cream-of-Shrimp Soup
Stuffed Pear Salad*
Bread Sticks
Chocolate Angel-Food Cake   Hot Tea

STUFFED PEAR SALAD

2 3-ounce packages cream cheese, softened	1 cup canned diced, roasted almonds
2 cups creamed cottage cheese	Salad greens
	8 fresh pears
1 cup snipped, pitted dates	Lemon juice

Early on day:
1. In bowl combine cream cheese, cottage cheese, dates, and almonds; refrigerate.
2. Wash and refrigerate salad greens.

About 30 minutes before serving:
1. Pare, halve, then scoop out centers of pears. Sprinkle generously with lemon juice.
2. Arrange 2 pear halves on salad greens on each salad plate. Fill each pear half with fruited cheese mixture. Makes 8 servings.

PATIO LUNCHEON
Fruit Cooler in Frosted Glasses with Fresh Mint Sprigs
Summery Chicken Salad*
Broccoli Spears topped with Buttered Baby Peas
Stewed Purple Plums with Sour Cream and Nutmeg
Iced Tea

SUMMERY CHICKEN SALAD

3 cups cooked chicken, cut in large pieces	½ cup mayonnaise or cooked salad dressing
1 cup celery, cut on diagonal	¼ cup commercial sour cream
½ cup simple French dressing	1 3¾-ounce package potato chips
½ teaspoon salt	½ cup grated process Cheddar cheese
¼ teaspoon pepper	

Day before, or early on day:
In medium bowl combine chicken and celery; stir in French dressing, salt, and pepper; refrigerate.

About 20 minutes before serving:
1. Preheat broiler 10 minutes, or as manufacturer directs.
2. Combine mayonnaise and sour cream; toss with drained chicken and celery mixture; pile in center of 9-inch pie plate. Stand potato chips, on edge, around inside edge of pie plate. Sprinkle grated cheese around base of chicken salad.
3. Quickly broil until cheese melts and potato chips "toast" a bit around edges. Serve at once. Makes 4 or 5 generous luncheon servings.

LUNCHEON FOR THE GARDEN CLUB
Hot Bouillon
Jambon à la Mousse*
Hot Whole-Wheat Rolls
Lime Sherbet with Fresh Strawberry Garnish
Hot Tea

JAMBON À LA MOUSSE

2 envelopes unflavored gelatin	1 cup heavy cream, whipped
¼ cup cold water	3 hard-cooked eggs, quartered
1 cup boiling water	
2 chicken-bouillon cubes	Lettuce
2 tablespoons canned tomato sauce	½ cup mayonnaise or cooked salad dressing
2 4½-ounce cans deviled ham	¼ cup diced green pepper
	¼ cup diced celery
	1 tablespoon lemon juice

Day before:
1. Soften gelatin in cold water; stir in boiling water and bouillon cubes; continue to stir until dissolved. Blend ⅓ cup of this hot mixture with tomato sauce, then pour into 1½-quart mold; refrigerate until firm.
2. Into remaining gelatin mixture stir deviled ham until smooth. Fold in whipped cream; refrigerate.
3. When tomato mixture is set, fill mold with deviled-ham mixture; refrigerate.

Just before serving, next day:
1. Unmold deviled-ham mixture on serving plate; decorate with hard-cooked eggs and lettuce; refrigerate.
2. In small serving bowl, mix mayonnaise, green pepper, celery, and lemon juice; refrigerate.
3. Serve mousse, cut into 8 wedges; pass mayonnaise. Makes 8 servings.

SALAD SPECTACULAR
Fruited Apricot Mold*
Deviled Ham Fan Tans
Celery Curls   Ripe Olives
Mint Brownies à la Mode   Hot or Iced Coffee

FRUITED APRICOT MOLD

1 package orange-flavor gelatin	2 tablespoons lemon juice
1 envelope unflavored gelatin	3 oranges, sectioned
	1 1-pound 4½-ounce can pineapple chunks
2 tablespoons granulated sugar	1 1-pound 1-ounce can spiced grapes, drained
¾ cup water	Boston lettuce
1 12-ounce can apricot nectar	1 8-ounce package cream cheese

Day before:
1. In saucepan combine orange gelatin and unflavored

Crown Tart

Cheese-Souffléd Tomatoes

gelatin with sugar. Stir in water and apricot nectar; heat, over low heat, stirring, until gelatins are completely dissolved. Add lemon juice; refrigerate.

2. In bottom of 2-quart ring mold arrange orange sections. Sprinkle with drained pineapple chunks (reserve syrup) and grapes. Pour on apricot gelatin mixture; refrigerate overnight.

About 15 minutes before serving:

1. Quickly dip mold in and out of warm water up to ½ inch of top. Invert serving dish on top; invert both; gently shake until salad slips out. Garnish with lettuce.

2. With mixer, beat cream cheese until soft; beat in enough reserved pineapple syrup to make of dressing consistency. Serve over salad. Makes 6 servings.

GOURMET-CLUB LUNCHEON
*Crown Tart**
Fresh-Fruit Salad
Gingersnaps
Hot Coffee or Tea

CROWN TART

1 package piecrust mix	¼ teaspoon paprika
Butter or margarine	½ cup heavy cream,
2 4-ounce packages Danish	whipped
blue cheese, coarsely	2 tablespoons snipped
grated	chives
¼ cup sherry	Fresh dill
2 3-ounce packages cream	Tiny candles (optional)
cheese	

1. Prepare piecrust mix as package label directs; then use half of it to make and bake a 9-inch pasty shell. Cool; then loosen pastry edges from pie plate so finished tart will slip out easily at serving time.

2. Using stockinet-covered rolling pin and floured pastry cloth, roll out rest of pastry into a 6½-by-4-inch rectangle. Spread with 3 tablespoons butter to within ½ inch of edges, then fold in thirds to form a three-layered rectangle; wrap in wax paper; refrigerate about 15 minutes. Repeat this rolling, folding, and chilling procedure 3 times more. Then, after last rolling and folding, refrigerate pastry for at least 30 minutes.

3. Now roll chilled pastry into an 8½-inch circle, ⅛ inch thick; place on ungreased cookie sheet; then with small, sharp knife, cut scallops all around its outer edge.

4. With tiny cookie cutter or knife, cut a ½-inch circle in center of pastry, but do not remove it. Then, with knife, mark 2-inch "spokes" not all the way through pastry, equidistantly around center circle. Refrigerate 1 hour.

5. Now start heating oven to 475°F.

6. Bake pastry 12 to 15 minutes, or until puffed and golden-brown; cool on cookie sheet 2 minutes. With broad spatula transfer to wire rack; cool; then wrap carefully in saran.

7. In medium bowl, with mixer at low speed, blend blue cheese, cream cheese, ¼ cup butter, sherry, and paprika; beat at high speed until light and fluffy. With rubber spatula fold in whipped cream and chives. Spread this mixture evenly in pastry shell, reserving 1 teaspoon of it in a custard cup; refrigerate overnight.

At serving time:

1. Remove filled pastry shell from refrigerator; gently tip pie plate until tart begins to slide out; then steady bottom of it with free hand and set on serving dish. Now remove center from scalloped pastry crust; set crust in center of tart. Place reserved teaspoon of filling in center of crust; set pastry circle cutout on top. Garnish with dill sprigs *as pictured opposite.*

2. If candles are used, set them around outer edge of crust between scallops. With very sharp knife, cut tart into 10 wedges, supporting side of tart shell with free hand as you cut. Makes 10 servings.

SHOW-OFF TO PERFECTION
*Cheese-Souffléd Tomatoes**
Tossed Mixed Salad
Assorted Hot Breads
Chocolate-Mint Parfaits
Iced Tea

CHEESE-SOUFFLÉD TOMATOES

7 large firm tomatoes	¼ cup heavy cream
¼ cup butter or margarine	1½ cups grated natural
½ cup regular all-purpose	Swiss cheese, lightly
flour	packed
Salt	1½ cups cooked rice
Pepper	¼ cup snipped parsley
⅛ teaspoon nutmeg	4 eggs, separated
½ teaspoon seasoned salt	Few sprigs parsley
1 cup milk	

About 1 hour and 45 minutes before serving:

1. Wash tomatoes; from top of each cut off ½-inch-thick slice. Scoop out inside of each, being careful not to break skin; invert on paper towels to drain.

2. In medium saucepan melt butter; stir in flour, 1¼ teaspoons salt, ⅛ teaspoon pepper, nutmeg, and seasoned salt. Slowly add milk and cream, blending well. Cook, stirring constantly, until smooth and thickened; blend in grated cheese, reserving 2 tablespoons. Remove from heat and turn into large bowl. Stir in rice, parsley, then egg yolks, one at a time; let cool.

3. Start heating oven to 400°F.

4. Meanwhile, arrange tomatoes, top side up, in shallow 15-by-10-inch ovenproof platter. Sprinkle with salt and pepper. Now cut 7 strips of foil, each long enough to wrap around one tomato, and wide enough to stand

1½ inches above its top edge. Securely wrap each strip around a tomato, fastening with cellophane tape.

5. Beat egg whites until stiff, then fold into cooled cheese mixture. Now spoon this mixture into tomatoes, dividing it equally; sprinkle reserved cheese over top of cheese mixture.

6. Bake 40 minutes, or until soufflé mixture is puffy and golden. Carefully remove foil, loosening with a sharp knife; garnish with parsley. Serve at once *as pictured on page 6.* Makes 7 servings.

AN ORIENTAL TOUCH
Tomato or Pineapple Juice
*Chinese Chicken with Noodles**
Tossed Romaine Salad   Crisp Crackers
Jelly-Cake Roll
Hot Tea

CHINESE CHICKEN WITH NOODLES

2 tablespoons butter or margarine	⅛ teaspoon pepper
1 medium onion, thinly sliced	2 tablespoons soy sauce
2 cups coarsely-sliced cabbage	1 cup canned chicken broth
1 6-ounce can whole mushrooms, drained, quartered	1 10-ounce package frozen whole green beans
1 tablespoon cornstarch	2 cups cut-up cooked chicken
½ teaspoon salt	4 cups hot cooked noodles
	4 radishes, sliced
	1 scallion, cut up

About 30 minutes before serving:
1. In large skillet melt butter; in it sauté onion until golden; then add cabbage and mushrooms; sauté a few minutes.

2. In small bowl combine cornstarch, salt, pepper, soy sauce, and chicken broth, stirring until smooth. Pour over vegetables in skillet; add green beans and chicken; simmer, covered, 8 to 10 minutes, or until vegetables are tender-crisp.

3. Arrange seasoned noodles around edge of large serving dish. Heap chicken-vegetable mixture in center; garnish with radishes and scallion. Serve with more soy sauce, if desired. Makes 6 servings.

LUNCHEON ELEGANTE
*Breast of Chicken Périgourdine**
Buttered Peas
Salad of Boston Lettuce   French Bread
*Oranges in the Clouds**
Coffee or Tea

BREAST OF CHICKEN PÉRIGOURDINE

8 whole chicken breasts	2 tablespoons light cream
1½ cups chicken broth	2 egg yolks
Butter or margarine	¼ teaspoon salt
12 large fresh mushrooms, sliced	Dash cayenne pepper
⅓ cup regular all-purpose flour	½ cup melted butter or margarine
¼ teaspoon salt	1 tablespoon lemon juice
	3 tablespoons sherry

About 1 hour and 30 minutes before serving:
1. Bone chicken breasts, reserving bones.
2. Simmer chicken bones in chicken broth, covered, about 1 hour; discard bones, reserving broth.

Company Tuna-Rice Cones

3. In small amount of butter, in large, metal-handled skillet, gently brown chicken breasts on both sides, adding more butter as needed; remove. In more butter, in same skillet, sauté mushrooms until golden; remove.

4. Into drippings in same skillet, stir flour, ¼ teaspoon salt, broth (add water if necessary to measure 1½ cups), and cream. Cook, stirring, over medium heat until thickened and smooth. Place chicken breasts in sauce; simmer gently, covered, about 20 minutes, or until chicken is tender.

5. Meanwhile, preheat broiler 10 minutes, or as manufacturer directs. Also make Hollandaise sauce: In small bowl, with mixer, beat egg yolks until thick; add ¼ teaspoon salt and cayenne; add ¼ cup melted butter, about 1 teaspoon at a time, beating constantly. Combine remaining ¼ cup melted butter and lemon juice; slowly add, about 2 teaspoon at a time, to egg-yolk mixture, beating constantly. Refrigerate.

6. When chicken is tender, add sherry and mushrooms. Then, over chicken spread Hollandaise; run under broiler 1 minute, or until golden. Serve, garnished with parsley *as pictured on page 11*. Makes 8 servings.

ORANGES IN THE CLOUDS

5 teaspoons unflavored gelatin	2 teaspoons grated lemon or lime peel
1 cup cold water	½ cup lemon or lime juice
1½ cups granulated sugar	6 egg whites, unbeaten
⅛ teaspoon salt	Custard Sauce, below
1½ cups boiling water	Unpeeled orange slices, halved

Day before, or early on day:

1. In large bowl sprinkle gelatin over cold water to soften; add sugar, salt, and boiling water; stir until gelatin is dissolved. Add lemon peel and juice; stir until blended. Refrigerate, stirring often, until consistency of unbeaten egg white.

2. Meanwhile, make Custard Sauce.

3. When gelatin mixture has thickened, add egg whites. Then, with mixer at medium speed, beat until just beginning to hold shape and very frothy—about 15 minutes. Refrigerate.

At serving time:

Spoon gelatin mixture into serving bowl or sherbet glasses. Spoon some of Custard Sauce over top. Tuck halved orange slices here and there. Pass rest of Custard Sauce. Makes 8 to 10 servings.

CUSTARD SAUCE: Partially fill bottom of double boiler with water; set top in place; pour in 2 cups milk; cover. Heat milk until tiny bubbles appear around edge. In medium bowl, beat 6 egg yolks slightly with a fork, then stir in 3 to 4 tablespoons granulated sugar and ¼ teaspoon salt. Add hot milk *slowly*, stirring *constantly*, to avoid cooked egg specks. Pour sauce back into double-boiler. Cook over hot, not boiling, water, stirring constantly, until thick enough to coat a metal spoon. Remove at once and pour into cool bowl. Let cool, then add 1 teaspoon vanilla extract or ½ teaspoon almond extract; lay wax paper directly on surface; refrigerate.

COME ON FRIDAY
*Company Tuna-Rice Cones**
Romaine Salad
Sesame Bread Fingers
Almond-Vanilla Pudding with Chocolate Sauce
Hot Tea

COMPANY TUNA-RICE CONES

Butter or margarine	Lemon juice
¼ cup regular all-purpose flour	Granulated or brown sugar
1 cup milk	4 egg whites, slightly beaten
4 egg yolks, slightly beaten	2½ cups crushed corn flakes
½ cup grated process Cheddar cheese	Salad oil
4 cups cooked rice	4 10-ounce packages frozen broccoli spears
2 7-ounce cans tuna, drained, then flaked (2 cups)	2 10½-ounce cans condensed cream-of-mushroom soup, undiluted
2 teaspoons salt	Paprika (optional)
10 canned pineapple slices, drained	

Day before, or early on day:

1. In saucepan over low heat, melt ¼ cup butter. Stir in flour until blended, then milk. Cook, stirring, until a thickened, smooth sauce; pour into large bowl.

2. Into sauce stir egg yolks, cheese, rice, tuna, and salt; refrigerate.

About 1 hour before serving:

1. Place pineapple slices on cookie sheet; sprinkle with lemon juice; brush with some melted butter; sprinkle with sugar.

2. Shape tuna mixture into 10 cones. Dip each in egg whites, then roll in corn flakes until coated.

3. In large deep kettle, heat 1½ inches salad oil to 350°F. on deep-fat-frying thermometer. Preheat broiler 10 minutes, or as manufacturer directs.

4. Fry cones, 4 or 5 at a time, in hot oil until golden brown; drain on paper towels; keep warm.

5. Meanwhile, cook broccoli as package labels direct. Also broil pineapple slices, 3 to 4 inches from heat, 8 minutes, or until golden. Heat mushroom soup.

6. On large heated platter arrange border of pineapple slices; then top each with a cone, spoon on mushroom soup, sprinkle with paprika. Then arrange broccoli in center *as pictured opposite*. Pass remaining mushroom soup. Makes 8 to 10 servings.

GOOD-NEIGHBORLY MEXICAN LUNCHEON
Gazpacho*
Shrimp a "La Cocina"*
Endive with Oil and Vinegar Dressing
Hot Rolls
Raspberry Meringue*   *Coffee*

GAZPACHO

2 onions, cut up	1 10½-ounce can con-
2 small cloves garlic	densed beef bouillon,
5 tomatoes	undiluted
4 green peppers, seeded	1 teaspoon diced green
2 teaspoons salt	pepper
½ teaspoon pepper	1 teaspoon diced radishes
2 teaspoons paprika	1 teaspoon diced cucumber
⅓ cup olive oil	Croutons
⅓ cup wine vinegar	

Early on day:

1. In blender container place onions, garlic, and 1 tomato, quartered; cover and blend at high speed until smooth; pour into bowl.
2. Blend 2 green peppers, cut into pieces, and 2 tomatoes, quartered, until smooth; pour into same bowl.
3. Blend remaining green peppers and tomatoes; add salt, pepper, paprika, then olive oil; pour into bowl. Stir in vinegar and beef bouillon; refrigerate.
4. Serve soup cold, topped with diced green pepper, radishes, and cucumbers, then croutons. Makes 8 servings.

SHRIMP A "LA COCINA"

12 deviled-egg halves	1 teaspoon salt
Butter or margarine	¼ teaspoon pepper
½ pound small mushrooms	2½ cups milk
1½ pounds shelled,	1 cup shredded Cheddar
deveined, raw shrimp	cheese
¼ cup regular all-purpose	3 slices bread, diced
flour	

Early on day:

1. In buttered 13-by-19-by-2-inch baking dish arrange deviled-egg halves.
2. In 2 tablespoons butter, in skillet, sauté mushrooms until golden; spoon over eggs; top with shrimp, halved if large.
3. In saucepan melt ¼ cup butter; stir in flour, salt, pepper, and milk; cook until thickened. Stir in cheese; pour over shrimp.
4. Sauté diced bread in 2 tablespoons butter; use to top shrimp. Refrigerate.

About 45 minutes before serving:

1. Start heating oven to 350°F.
2. Bake shrimp 35 minutes, or until hot. Makes 8 servings.

RASPBERRY MERINGUE

6 egg whites	1 cup heavy cream, whipped
½ teaspoon cream of	2 10-ounce packages frozen
tartar	raspberries, thawed,
Pinch salt	well drained
1 teaspoon vanilla extract	2 tablespoons sherry
1½ cups granulated sugar	(optional)

Early on day:

1. Start heating oven to 275°F. On cookie sheets, place 2 9-inch brown-paper circles.
2. Beat egg whites until very stiff and dry; quickly beat in cream of tartar, salt, vanilla, and sugar. Spread on paper circles.
3. Bake 30 minutes, then turn oven down to 225°F. and bake 45 minutes longer, or until soft layers lift easily from paper; cool.

At serving time:

Stack layers on cake plate. Fold raspberries into whipped cream with sherry, if desired. Heap on top of layers. Makes 12 servings.

STOP BY FOR CHOWDER
Long Island Fish Chowder*
A Basket of Pilot Crackers
Dark Green Salad with Sharp French Dressing*
Apricot-Cheese Pastry Hearts*
Coffee

LONG ISLAND FISH CHOWDER

2 kinds of fish—halibut,	½ cup finely-diced salt
whole sea bass, or	pork
whole flounder—each	4 medium potatoes, pared
weighing 2 pounds	5 medium onions, thinly
12 hard-shell clams,	sliced
shucked, in their juice	4 teaspoons salt
½ pound shrimp, shelled,	¼ teaspoon pepper
deveined	1 pint half-and-half
3 whole peppercorns	2 tablespoons regular all-
1 stalk celery	purpose flour
	¼ cup cold water

Have whole fish filleted and ask for bones, skin, and heads.

About 1 hour and 30 minutes before serving:

1. Place bones, skin, and heads in 6-quart Dutch oven or kettle; add water to cover, peppercorns, and celery. Simmer, covered, 30 minutes.
2. Meanwhile, sauté salt pork in skillet until each piece is golden-brown.
3. Strain fish stock, discarding bones, etc.; return stock to Dutch oven. Add potatoes, onions, and drippings from salt pork, reserving crisp bits. If necessary, add enough water to just cover potatoes. Add fish, cut into 2-inch pieces, clams, chopped, and their liquid,

Breast of Chicken Périgourdine

Apricot-Cheese Pastry Hearts

and shrimp. Sprinkle with salt and pepper. Simmer, covered, 20 minutes.

4. Now add half-and-half. Mix flour with water until smooth. Add to chowder. Cook for 8 to 10 minutes, or until fish and potatoes are just tender. Sprinkle pork bits over top. Makes 6 main-dish servings.

DARK GREEN SALAD WITH SHARP FRENCH DRESSING

2 heads Bibb lettuce or 1 medium head Boston lettuce	¾ teaspoon dry mustard ¼ teaspoon freshly-ground black pepper or ¼ teaspoon seasoned pepper
1 bunch water cress	¼ cup olive oil
1 clove garlic	1 tablespoon vinegar
¾ teaspoon salt	

Early on day:
Wash lettuce and water cress; break leaves into large pieces; refrigerate.
Just before serving:
1. Cut up garlic clove right into salad bowl. Next add salt, mustard, and pepper. Now, with back of spoon, mash seasonings together until garlic is pulverized. Into this, with fork, stir olive oil, then vinegar. Top with 2 quarts of salad greens, but don't toss. Refrigerate until needed.
2. At salad time, whisk to table; toss well. Makes 6 servings.

APRICOT-CHEESE PASTRY HEARTS

1 cup sifted regular all-purpose flour	½ 8-ounce package cream cheese
⅛ teaspoon salt	Apricot or raspberry preserves
½ cup butter or margarine	1 egg, beaten

Day before, if desired:
Into medium bowl sift flour and salt; add butter and cream cheese, in small pieces. With pastry blender, or 2 knives, cut butter and cheese into flour until all is well blended. Shape into ball; wrap in wax paper, saran, or foil, then refrigerate.
Early on day, or about 2 hours before serving:
1. Lightly grease 2 cookie sheets. Start heating oven to 400°F.
2. On floured surface, roll out dough ⅛ inch thick. Then with 3-by-2¾-inch heart-shaped cookie cutter, cut out hearts. Remove trimmings; reroll and cut out once or twice more.
3. In center of half of pastry hearts, place 1 scant teaspoonful of preserves. Now brush their edges with beaten egg; cover each with another cutout heart; then, with fork, press edges together. Arrange on cookie sheet. Brush top of each heart with beaten egg; sprinkle each with granulated sugar, if desired.

4. Bake 10 to 12 minutes, or until golden; cool on wire racks. Makes about 24.

For a new look: Roll out dough into 2 9-inch circles; with sharp knife, cut out 2 large hearts or other design *as pictured on page 11.* Over one of hearts spread preserves, to within ½ inch of edge. Brush edge with beaten egg. Top with second pastry heart, pressing edges together in scalloped effect. Place small cutouts on top, if desired. Brush top with beaten egg; with large spatula transfer to cookie sheet. Bake 15 minutes, or until golden; cool on wire rack. Brush top with preserves, if desired. To serve, cut into wedges.

A DESSERT LUNCHEON
Omelet Coeur à la Crème*
Hot Coffee

OMELET COEUR À LA CRÈME

½ 3-ounce package cream cheese	1 teaspoon salt
½ cup creamed cottage cheese	1½ tablespoons butter or margarine
1 teaspoon grated orange peel	Confectioners' sugar
Granulated sugar	1 10-ounce package frozen sliced strawberries, thawed
8 eggs	Fresh strawberries (optional)
1 tablespoon cold water	

Day before, if desired:
In small bowl, rub cream cheese with back of spoon against side of bowl until soft; stir in cottage cheese, orange peel, and 2 teaspoons granulated sugar. In another bowl place eggs, water, salt, and 2 teaspoons granulated sugar. Refrigerate both bowls.
At serving time:
1. Melt butter in 10-inch skillet. Then tip skillet back and forth to grease bottom and sides thoroughly. With mixer, blend egg mixture well. Pour into hot greased skillet.
2. As mixture sets at edges, gently pull in toward center with rubber spatula or fork, letting uncooked mixture flow to bottom. Repeat around omelet. Continue until all of omelet is creamy, *not dry,* though rough on top.
3. With cheese mixture, cover half of omelet away from handle. With skillet tilted at 45° angle in left hand, fold uncovered half over cheese.
4. Now hold skillet with left hand, and platter with right hand so edge of skillet rests on edge of platter. Slowly tip together until omelet rolls out on platter. Sprinkle omelet with confectioners' sugar, then spoon on thawed frozen strawberries. Garnish with fresh berries, if desired.
5. Serve omelet at once, passing rest of frozen berries. Makes 4 luncheon main-dish or dessert servings.

The usual male criticism of an otherwise popular way to dine is, "But where can I put down my plate?" In answer to this agonized query we have designed the sit-down buffet—both convenient and charming for host and hostess, male and female guests. §Whether you set up your buffet on a second table in the living

Sit-Down Buffets Men Will Like

room, breakfast room, or at one end of the dining room, or use a sideboard, your guests can seat themselves at the dining room table in comfort. And if your table isn't large enough for everyone, set up card tables. §Set the sit-down table with napkins, main-course silver, and water glasses. You may want to add bread-and-butter plates. Some hostesses prefer to place the dessert silver on the table from the start. Its placement is above the space for the dinner plate, horizontally, with the fork handle to the left and spoon handle to the right. (See the diagram below.) The first course may be served in the living room—or it may be set in place at the dinner table. When finished, while the hostess clears, the guests go on to the buffet for the main course.

HOW TO SET UP A BUFFET

Whether you've chosen a second table or a sideboard, low bookcase, or chest of drawers for your buffet, it's essential that it be set up in logical serving order so that your guests can move around easily. The situation of your buffet will depend on the number of guests and the layout of your room. Shown below are two plans that may be readily adapted to your buffet—a buffet table against a wall, and one in the center of the room. Food, china, and other table furnishings should be in this order: dinner plates, hot dishes or cold dishes (either one first, whichever you prefer), salad, bread, relishes. Be sure that each food has its own serving silver beside or in it. If possible, leave enough room near each dish so that guests won't have to perform an awkward balancing act, but can put down their plates and serve themselves easily. Please: warm your plates for hot foods just as you would for a regular sit-down dinner. Keep hot foods hot in chafing dishes, electric casseroles, or on a candle-warmer or hot-plate tray.

A HELPING HAND

Since the aim of our sit-down buffets is comfort with no loss of graciousness, the host could serve the meat or salad to each guest at the buffet table. And there's no rule against the hostess serving the vegetables! If you decide to engage a maid for the occasion, she helps the guests at the buffet. Often a good friend can be recruited for this duty (and also be prevailed upon to help clear afterwards).

THE SWEET CONCLUSION

Dinner's end may take several forms. You might arrange to have that good friend remove the main-course plates while you clear the buffet table and reset it with dessert and dessert plates, silver and a coffee service. Some find it simpler to set up the dessert before hand on a side table from which the guests help themselves. Or place the desserts on plates in the kitchen and then serve. Many hostesses prefer to arrange everything on trays in the kitchen: dessert on one tray, coffee on another. With the dessert tray in front of you on the dining table and the coffee on a hostess cart or low table to your right, you're ready to serve.

SOME POINTERS FOR BUFFET HOSTESSES

There may be a guest or two who like their coffee with the main course. As an alternative to the suggestions above, the coffee service plus water pitcher and glasses may be set up on a side table, available to guests all during the meal. / Casseroles are an easy main dish. (You can cook and serve from the same dish—and a second casserole may be kept warm for second helpings.) Whatever the dish, watch to see that there is enough for all and replenish food when necessary. / Prebuttering the bread is a good way to speed up service and dispense with bread-and-butter plates and butter spreaders. / Starred recipes (*) in our buffet menus appear below them.

14

·BEAUTIFULLY INFORMAL
Lemony Chicken Soup*
Calico Salad*
Pumpernickel Bread
Apple Pie with Cheese Wedges   *Coffee*

LEMONY CHICKEN SOUP

2 10½-ounce cans con- densed chicken-with-rice soup, undiluted	3 to 4 drops yellow food color (optional) Fresh lemon slices
2 soup-cans water	Snipped fresh dill
4 eggs	(optional)
2 tablespoons lemon juice	

About 20 minutes before serving:

1. In large saucepan blend soup with water; heat to boiling, then simmer a few minutes.
2. Meanwhile, in small bowl, beat eggs with lemon juice until thick—about 10 minutes. Now, add a little hot soup to egg mixture, stirring constantly.
3. Remove remaining soup from heat; slowly stir in egg mixture; blend in food color to tint delicate yellow. Serve at once, garnished with lemon slices and dill *as pictured opposite.* Makes 6 to 8 servings.

CALICO SALAD

Swedish Meat Balls, below	3 4-ounce cans Vienna
Tongue Salad, below	sausages
Green-Pepper Salad, below	Butter or margarine
Coleslaw, below	Pumpernickel bread
1 large red onion	

Several days ahead:

Make Swedish Meat Balls; then freezer-wrap them and freeze until time to thaw and heat as directed.

Early on day:

1. Transfer frozen meat balls to refrigerator to thaw.
2. Prepare Tongue Salad; refrigerate. Prepare Green-Pepper Salad; refrigerate. Finely shred cabbage for Coleslaw; refrigerate. Thinly slice red onion; wrap in saran or foil; refrigerate.
3. Drain Vienna sausages; refrigerate. Shape ¼ pound butter into 8 balls; arrange on small plate, cover with saran or foil, and refrigerate.

About 30 minutes before serving:

1. In 1 to 2 tablespoons hot butter, in skillet, over medium heat, heat meat balls, covered, turning often.
2. In 2 tablespoons melted butter, in another skillet, sauté Vienna sausages, until light brown and hot, turning them occasionally.
3. Meanwhile, complete Coleslaw as directed.
4. Then, on large serving tray, starting at far right-hand corner, mound drained Coleslaw, next drained Green-Pepper Salad, then red-onion rings.
5. In middle row mound drained Vienna sausages,

drained Swedish Meat Balls, then drained Tongue Salad. Then halve pumpernickel-bread slices and arrange as an outer row, with a few buttered halves in front as *pictured opposite.*

6. Place tray on buffet with butter balls. Guests help themselves. Makes 6 servings.

Swedish Meat Balls

Butter or margarine	½ teaspoon allspice
⅓ cup chopped onion	¼ teaspoon nutmeg
1 egg	¼ teaspoon pepper
½ cup milk	1 pound chuck, ground
½ cup fresh bread crumbs	¼ pound pork shoulder,
1¼ teaspoons salt	ground
2 teaspoons granulated	
sugar	

1. In 2 tablespoons hot butter, in large skillet, sauté onion until golden. Meanwhile, in large bowl lightly beat egg; add milk and bread crumbs. Let this mixture stand 5 minutes.
2. Then, to egg add salt, sugar, allspice, nutmeg, pepper, chuck, pork, and onion mixture. Blend with fork. Shape mixture into 1-inch balls.
3. In 2 tablespoons hot butter, in same skillet, brown meat balls well on all sides; then simmer until done— about 5 minutes. Cool; then freezer-wrap and freeze until time to thaw and heat in 1 to 2 tablespoons hot butter, covered, turning often. Makes about 18.

Tongue Salad

6 cooked tongue slices, ¼ inch thick	½ cup French dressing

Early on day:

Cut tongue slices into lengthwise strips ¼ inch wide. Toss them with French dressing, then cover and refrigerate. Make 3 cups.

Green-Pepper Salad

3 large green peppers, seeded	⅓ cup Italian dressing

Early on day:

Cut green peppers into ¼-inch dice (2½ cups); toss with Italian dressing. Cover; refrigerate. Makes 2½ cups.

Coleslaw

1 quart finely-shredded green cabbage	⅓ cup Italian dressing

Early on day:

Prepare cabbage, then refrigerate.

Just before serving:

Lightly toss cabbage with Italian dressing. Makes 1 quart.

Roast-Beef-Hearty Party Salad

Fresh Tomato Soufflé

Curried-Rice Meat-Ball Casserole

Lemony Chicken Soup, Calico Salad

GATHERING OF THE CLAN
Rock Cornish Hens* on Rice Mingle*
with Bordelaise Sauce*
Mushrooms à la Crème*
Green Beans with Onions   Parslied Peas
Shredded-Beet Salad   Braided Bread
Almond Puffs*   Epergne of Fruits and Sweetmeats
Demitasse

ROCK CORNISH HENS ON RICE MINGLE

8 frozen Rock Cornish hens (about 1 pound each)	1/4 cup melted butter or margarine
Salt	Rice Mingle, below
Pepper	Bordelaise Sauce, below
Soft butter or margarine	Bunchlets fresh green grapes
Paprika	

Day before:
Remove hens from freezer; place on large deep platter or metal tray in refrigerator to thaw.
Early on day:
Remove giblets from hens; then wash and dry them. Sprinkle hens with salt and pepper; with thin string tie legs together. Rub hens with soft butter; sprinkle with paprika. Place in shallow open roasting pan, then refrigerate.
About 1 hour and 15 minutes before serving:
1.   Start heating oven to 425°F.
2.   Roast hens, uncovered, about 1 hour, or until tender and well browned, basting with melted butter.
3.   Meanwhile, start cooking Rice Mingle. Also prepare step 1 of Bordelaise Sauce.
4.   When hens are done, cut and remove string. Arrange them on heated platter, piled high in center with Rice Mingle. Arrange bunchlets of grapes on top of hens; keep warm.
5.   Complete Bordelaise Sauce. Then let guests help themselves to hens, rice, and sauce. Makes 8 servings.

RICE MINGLE

1 cup wild rice	2 10½-ounce cans condensed beef consommé, undiluted
Salt	
2 cups boiling water	
Butter or margarine	2 cups uncooked regular white rice
2 medium onions, minced	Dash pepper

About 50 minutes before serving:
1.   Wash wild rice in 2 or 3 changes of cold water, removing foreign particles.
2.   In medium saucepan, add 1 teaspoon salt to boiling water; add wild rice gradually so water keeps boiling. Boil, covered, stirring occasionally with fork, 30 to 45 minutes, or until rice is just tender.
3.   Meanwhile, in 1/4 cup butter, in deep 10-inch skillet, over medium heat, sauté onions about 5 minutes. Then, with fork, stir in consommé, 1 soup-can water, white rice, and ½ teaspoon salt. Cover skillet tightly. Bring to boil, reduce heat, then simmer about 20 minutes, or until rice is tender and all liquid absorbed. Four or five times during cooking stir rice with fork to prevent sticking.
4.   To drained wild rice add 1 tablespoon butter and dash pepper. Then, with fork, fluff it up, add cooked white rice and toss together. Heap lightly in center of platter with Cornish hens around it. Makes about 8 servings.

BORDELAISE SAUCE

½ teaspoon dried whole thyme	1/3 cup boiling water
1 bay leaf	1 tablespoon cornstarch
1 cup port wine	2 teaspoons granulated sugar
2 chicken-bouillon cubes	1 medium onion, chopped

1.   In small bowl combine thyme, bay leaf, and wine; set aside. Dissolve bouillon cubes in boiling water; stir in cornstarch and sugar; set aside.
2.   When Cornish hens are done and have been arranged on serving platter, pour one-half of the hot drippings from roasting pan into small skillet. In drippings, sauté onion 5 minutes. Stir in cornstarch mixture; bring to boil. Stir in wine; simmer 5 minutes.
3.   Strain sauce into gravyboat, for guests to help themselves. Makes 8 servings.

MUSHROOMS À LA CRÈME

3 tablespoons butter or margarine	1 10½-ounce can condensed cream-of-mushroom soup, undiluted
1½ pounds medium fresh mushrooms	½ cup milk
3 tablespoons lemon juice	1 teaspoon salt
	½ teaspoon pepper

About 30 minutes before serving:
1.   In butter, in large skillet, over high heat, sauté mushrooms about 10 minutes, or until done. Add lemon juice and toss.
2.   Then add mushroom soup, milk, salt, and pepper; heat, stirring until smooth. Makes 8 servings.

ALMOND PUFFS

1 package active dry, or	2½ cups sifted regular
cake, yeast	all-purpose flour
¼ cup warm water	2 eggs
½ cup milk, scalded	½ cup finely-chopped
¼ cup butter or margarine	blanched almonds
Granulated sugar	⅓ cup finely-chopped
½ teaspoon salt	blanched almonds

Day before:
1. Dissolve yeast in warm water. In medium bowl combine milk, butter, 1 tablespoon sugar, and salt; cool to lukewarm.
2. Into cooled milk stir yeast and 2 cups flour; beat well with spoon. Add eggs, one at a time, beating well after each addition. Then add remaining flour and beat until batter is smooth. Cover and let rise in warm place until doubled in bulk—about 1 hour.
3. Start heating oven to 400°F.
4. Now, to batter add ½ cup almonds; beat well. Grease 16 2¼-inch cupcake-pans; spoon batter into cups until three-fourths full. Combine ⅓ cup almonds with 3 tablespoons sugar; use to sprinkle on top of each cup.
5. Bake about 20 minutes, or until golden. Remove from pan immediately; cool, then store.
Next day, just before serving:
Arrange puffs in baking pan; cover with foil. Reheat in 425°F. oven from which Cornish hens have just been taken, for about 10 minutes. Makes 16.

A MAN'S MENU
Roast-Beef-Hearty Party Salad*
Chilled Radishes
Crisp French Bread
Fruit-and-Cheese Tray
Iced Coffee

ROAST-BEEF-HEARTY PARTY SALAD

2 9-ounce packages frozen	¼ teaspoon dried parsley
French-style green beans	flakes
2 10-ounce packages frozen	¼ teaspoon dried mint
lima beans	¼ teaspoon orégano
1 pound small white turnips	1 cup Italian dressing
1 1-pound can whole tiny	1 4-pound sirloin tip roast
carrots	

Day before, if desired, or early on day:
1. Cook green beans and limas as package labels direct until just tender-crisp; drain. Prepare turnips, cutting them into quarters or sixths; cook until tender; drain.
2. Start heating oven to 325°F.
3. Toss together drained green beans, limas, turnips, and carrots. Sprinkle with parsley, mint, and orégano; pour on half of Italian dressing; toss well. Cover with foil or saran; refrigerate.

4. Roast meat, on rack, to desired degree of doneness, using a roast-meat thermometer. When done, cool in pan; wrap well in foil; refrigerate until next day.
About 20 minutes before serving:
1. Slice roast beef. Then use enough slightly overlapping slices to go around inside of 3- or 4-quart glass salad or punch bowl, placing them so they overhang about 1 inch at top *as pictured on page 15.* Any extra roast-beef slices may be arranged on a platter and served on the side.
2. Now heap marinated vegetables in center of bowl, piling them high. Serve, passing rest of Italian dressing in a pitcher. Makes 8 servings.

DO-AHEAD BUFFET
Cold Sliced Chicken
Fresh Tomato Soufflé* with Chive Mayonnaise
Bibb Lettuce, Green Onions, Ripe Olives
Herbed Melba Toast
Minted Pineapple Chunks
Iced Tea

FRESH TOMATO SOUFFLÉ

3 pounds ripe tomatoes	4½ teaspoons Worcester-
¼ cup salad oil	shire
2 tablespoons minced onion	1½ teaspoons Tabasco
1½ teaspoons crushed	4 envelopes plus 1½
garlic	teaspoons unflavored
1 teaspoon salt	gelatin
¼ teaspoon pepper	¾ cup water
1½ cups canned chicken	6 egg whites
broth	Skinned tomatoes (optional)
3 tablespoons canned	
tomato paste	

Day before:
1. Quarter washed tomatoes. In large saucepan heat salad oil; add tomatoes, onion, garlic, salt, and pepper. Boil, stirring occasionally, 5 minutes; add chicken broth, tomato paste, Worcestershire, and Tabasco. Simmer 4 minutes; remove from heat. Rub this mixture through sieve or food mill into large bowl.
2. Now, in measuring cup, sprinkle gelatin over water; set in small saucepan of hot water and stir until dissolved; add to tomato mixture. Refrigerate, stirring occasionally, until small amount mounds when dropped from spoon—about 1½ to 2 hours.
3. Meanwhile, fold a 30-inch length of foil, 12 inches wide, in half lengthwise. Wrap around outside of china soufflé dish, which measures 7½ cups to brim, so a collar 3 inches high stands above rim; fasten with cellophane tape; then tie tightly with thin string. Lightly oil inside of foil only.
5. Now, with mixer at high speed, beat chilled tomato mixture until fluffy and thick. Next beat egg whites

until stiff, but not dry. Fold them into tomato mixture. Pour into soufflé dish; refrigerate.

At serving time, next day:

1. Carefully remove foil collar from soufflé dish.
2. If desired, garnish top of soufflé with slices or wedges of skinned tomatoes *as pictured on page 15.* Makes 10 to 12 servings.

GALA BUFFET FOR VIPS

*Beef Wellington**
*Spinach Timbales on Tomato Rings**
Tall Green Salad
Radish Rose Tower
Petite Dinner Rolls
*Imperial Pears**
Hot Coffee

BEEF WELLINGTON

1½ times recipe Puff Paste, below
5- to 6-pound fillet of beef, trimmed of all fat
3 or 4 large pieces suet
2 tablespoons butter or margarine
4 chicken livers
½ pound fresh mushrooms, finely chopped
¼ pound cooked ham, finely ground
1 tablespoon catchup
⅓ cup sherry
1 egg, separated
Water cress

Several days before serving:

Make Puff Paste as directed; refrigerate, wrapped.

Day before serving:

1. Start heating oven to 425°F.
2. Place fillet on rack in roasting pan, then lay pieces of suet over it. Insert roast-meat thermometer into center of fillet.
3. Roast to desired degree of doneness, then remove from oven; remove suet; let fillet cool, then refrigerate it.
4. In hot butter, in skillet, sauté chicken livers until browned; then chop them fine; return to skillet and add mushrooms, ham, catchup, and sherry. Cook, stirring occasionally, 10 minutes. Cool; stir in beaten egg yolk; remove to bowl; cover with foil; refrigerate.

About 1 hour before serving:

1. On floured board, roll out three-fourths of Puff Paste into a square about 18 by 18 inches, or large enough to enclose fillet. Now lay bottom center of fillet along one edge of Puff Paste; over top of fillet pat chopped ham mixture; then lift one end of Puff Paste up and over fillet, overlapping both ends under it. Tuck in other ends firmly. Then lift fillet to large cookie sheet, seam side down.
2. Start heating oven to 425°F.
3. Roll out remaining Puff Paste; then with small cookie cutters, cut out such decorative shapes as leaves, flowers, and triangles, with which to trim fillet, making 18 in all.
4. Quickly brush pastry surface of fillet with slightly beaten egg white; then arrange decorative shapes on it and brush again with egg white.
5. Bake 30 to 40 minutes, or until pastry is golden. Then, with 2 broad spatulas, lift fillet to serving platter; garnish with water cress. In serving, cut into ½-inch thick slices. Makes 14 servings.

PUFF PASTE

2 cups sifted regular all-purpose flour
½ cup water
¾ teaspoon salt
¼ cup water
1 cup firm, but not hard, butter or margarine (½ pound)

Three days ahead:

1. Into large bowl sift flour. Make well in center. Add ½ cup water and salt; with fork, working quickly and lightly, mix all together, adding ¼ cup water as the ½ cup water is absorbed into flour; refrigerate 15 minutes.
2. Place Puff Paste on floured board and roll into rectangle about ¼ inch thick. Now shape butter into a flat square cake 1 inch thick. Place butter in center of paste, then fold paste over it, enclosing it in an envelope-like shape.
3. Now roll folded paste away from you, into a long, thin rectangle, as thin as possible without letting butter break through. Fold into thirds, then bring one end over the center third, and the other end over the first. (This rolling, folding, and turning is called a "turn.")
4. Do a second "turn" on dough, then refrigerate 20 minutes. Do two more "turns," then refrigerate dough 30 minutes. Do two final "turns;" wrap paste in foil, then refrigerate until used.

HERB PUFF PASTE: Combine 1 tablespoon each of dried dill and tarragon with 1 tablespoon snipped parsley; sprinkle over Puff Paste before folding in step 3. Complete as directed.

SPINACH TIMBALES ON TOMATO RINGS

2 10-ounce packages frozen chopped spinach
Butter or margarine
6 eggs, slightly beaten
1⅓ cups milk
2 medium onions, grated
Salt
Pepper
1 tablespoon white vinegar
¼ teaspoon dried savory
8 tomato slices, about 2½ inches by ¼ inch

About 1 hour and 55 minutes before serving:

1. Cook spinach as package labels direct; drain *very* well. In medium bowl combine spinach, 3 tablespoons melted butter, eggs, milk, onions, 1¼ teaspoons salt, ¼ teaspoon pepper, vinegar, and savory.
2. Start heating oven to 350°F.
3. Generously butter 8 6-ounce custard cups. Divide spinach mixture evenly between them. Place cups in shallow roasting pan, in 1 inch hot water.

4. Bake 35 to 40 minutes, or until custard is set. Then remove pan from oven; wrap sheet of foil over and around custards, then let stand where they will keep warm until Beef Wellington is nearly done.

About 10 minutes before serving:

1. Sprinkle tomato slices with salt and pepper, or with seasoned salt and pepper, if desired.

2. Uncover roasting pan; with small spatula loosen each spinach mold all around. Lay salted side of tomato slice over top of custard cup; invert cup so spinach molds slips out onto tomato slice. Set on serving platter; repeat with rest of cups. Makes 8 servings.

IMPERIAL PEARS

2 packages regular vanilla- pudding-and-pie-filling mix
2 cups milk
2 cups light cream
2 tablespoons vanilla extract

9 medium ripe pears, with stems
1¾ cups granulated sugar
¼ cup lemon juice
¼ cup butter or margarine
2 cups boiling water
2 teaspoons almond extract

Anytime on day before:

1. In medium saucepan combine pudding mix with milk and cream; cook as package labels direct. Then remove from heat and stir in vanilla.

2. Pour sauce into medium bowl; place sheet of wax paper directly on surface of sauce; refrigerate.

Early on day, or 3 hours before serving:

1. Pare pears, leaving stems intact. Arrange pears, standing upright, in 3-quart casserole or shallow roasting pan.

2. Start heating oven to 350°F.

3. In saucepan simmer 1 cup sugar with lemon juice, butter, and boiling water 5 minutes. Remove from heat; stir in almond extract, then pour over pears.

4. Bake, covered, basting occasionally, 60 minutes, or until pears are just fork-tender. Uncover; drain; cool, then refrigerate.

About 20 minutes before serving:

1. Cover cookie sheet with double thickness of wax paper. Arrange baked, chilled pears on cookie sheet. (To insure that pears will stand upright, cut a small slice from bottom of each.)

2. In small saucepan, over medium heat, melt ¾ cup sugar until it becomes a clear golden syrup, stirring constantly; remove at once from heat. Quickly, but carefully, spoon syrup over each pear as a glaze.

3. While glaze hardens, spoon some of sauce into a chafing dish or serving dish; then, with broad spatula or pancake turner, lift each glazed pear and set upright in sauce *as pictured on page 26.*

4. Each guest spoons some of sauce into his deep sherbet or nappy dish, then tops with a pear. While eating it with a spoon, he holds pear by stem with other hand. Pass extra sauce. Makes 9 servings.

HOUSEWARMING BUFFET
Chicken Kahana* on Hot, Fluffy Rice
Mixed Tossed Salad
Coconut Layer Cake
Hot Coffee

CHICKEN KAHANA

⅓ cup regular all-purpose flour
¼ teaspoon ginger
1 teaspoon salt
1 3½- to 4-pound broiler- fryer, cut up
⅓ cup butter or margarine
⅓ cup water
1½ tablespoons cornstarch
¼ teaspoon curry powder

1 teaspoon instant minced onion
1 tablespoon catchup
1 13¾-ounce can chicken broth, undiluted
1 medium green pepper
1 small cantaloupe
1 5-ounce can water chestnuts, drained
3 cups hot, cooked rice

About 1 hour and 15 minutes before serving:

1. Mix flour, ginger, and salt; use to coat chicken, reserving any leftover flour mixture.

2. In hot butter, in large skillet, brown chicken pieces on all sides; sprinkle on reserved flour, then add water; cook, covered, 40 minutes, or until chicken is tender.

3. Meanwhile, combine cornstarch, curry powder, minced onion, and catchup. Slowly add part of chicken broth, stirring until smooth; stir in rest of broth; set aside.

4. Quarter, then seed, green pepper; cut it into thin slivers. Cut cantaloupe in half; scoop out seeds; then, with melon-ball cutter, or the ½ teaspoon of measuring-spoon set, scoop out cantaloupe balls. Thinly slice water chestnuts.

5. When tender, arrange chicken in center of warm platter; keep warm. Into drippings in skillet, stir broth mixture; cook, stirring constantly, until thickened. Add green-pepper slivers and water chestnuts; simmer until they are hot, then add cantaloupe balls.

6. Onto chicken spoon vegetables, melon balls, some of gravy; surround with rice. Pass rest of gravy. Makes 6 servings.

Summer-Supper Buffet

SUMMER-SUPPER BUFFET
Tuna-Lobster Cheese Ring*
Fruits Alaska*   *Minted Iced Tea*

TUNA-LOBSTER CHEESE RING

¾ cup butter or margarine
1½ cups water
Salt
1½ cups sifted regular all-purpose
   flour
6 eggs
Grated natural Swiss cheese
1 egg, beaten
2 cups cut-up celery
½ cup green-pepper strips
2 sliced scallions
1 4-ounce can pimentos, chopped
8 stuffed olives, halved

4 6½- or 7-ounce cans tuna, well
   drained
¾ pound cooked lobster meat, in
   chunks (2¼ cups)
1 teaspoon monosodium glutamate
½ teaspoon pepper
3 tablespoons lemon juice
¼ cup snipped dill
1¼ cups mayonnaise
6 radish roses
Lettuce leaves
Ripe olives

Day before:
1. In large saucepan combine butter, water, and ¾ teaspoon salt; bring to boil; stir to melt butter. Turn heat low; add flour; stir vigorously until dough leaves sides of pan in ball; remove from heat.
2. With mixer at medium speed, beat in 6 eggs, 2 at a time, until dough is shiny and smooth. Stir in 1 cup grated cheese.
3. Start heating oven to 400°F.
4. On cookie sheet draw a 12-inch circle; spread dough in a ring 2½ inches wide, just within drawn circle. Brush dough with beaten egg.
5. Bake 45 minutes; then turn oven temperature to 300°F. and bake 45 minutes longer. Cool ring on wire rack; wrap in foil.
6. While cheese ring bakes, prepare filling: In large bowl combine celery, green-pepper strips, scallions, pimentos, stuffed olives, tuna, lobster, 1½ teaspoons salt, monosodium glutamate, pepper, lemon juice, dill, and mayonnaise. Also prepare radish roses. Refrigerate all.
About 30 minutes before serving:
1. Split cheese ring horizontally; set bottom on platter. Top with tuna-lobster filling, lifted from juice, placing a few pieces lobster, red-side out, along outer edge of ring. Over filling lay a few lettuce leaves, then top of ring.
2. Tuck lettuce leaves under ring; sprinkle top with grated Swiss cheese. Garnish with radish roses and ripe olives *as pictured*. Refrigerate until ready to serve. Makes 12 servings.

FRUITS ALASKA

6 or 8 firm, favorite ice creams
   (allow ½ pint per serving)

Assortment of whole and cut
   favorite fruits

Early on day:
1. Cut containers from ice creams. Place ice creams on cookie sheet in freezer. (If desired, also pack ice creams into 6- and 8-ounce paper cups; freeze; then cut away paper cups and place on cookie sheet.)
2. Border large serving tray with fruits; refrigerate.
At dessert time:
With help of wide spatula, arrange ice creams on fruit-bordered tray, with some of fruits between ice creams *as pictured*.

NEW-LOOK BUFFET SUPPER
*Oven-Fried Drumsticks**
*Dilled Peas with Artichoke Hearts**
*Chive-Buttered Corn on the Cob**
*Sour-Cream Slaw**
Assorted Bread Tray:
Pumpernickel Sandwiches, Toasted English Muffins,
Corn Toasties, and Sesame Sticks
Vanilla-Ice-Cream and Orange-Sherbet Balls with
Chocolate Sauce
Sparkling Grape Juice or Lemonade

OVEN-FRIED DRUMSTICKS

24 chicken legs (drumsticks only)	2 teaspoons paprika
	1 teaspoon curry powder
½ cup regular all-purpose flour	3 teaspoons poultry seasoning
2¾ teaspoons salt	½ cup butter or margarine
½ teaspoon pepper	

About 1 hour and 15 minutes before serving:
1. Start heating oven to 450°F.
2. Push skin of each chicken leg up over broad cut end. In heavy brown paper bag combine flour, salt, pepper, paprika, curry powder, and poultry seasoning.
3. Fashion 2 pans each 13-by-9-by-1-inch from double thickness of regular foil or single thickness of heavy-duty foil. Lay each on cookie sheet; place ¼ cup butter in each; set in oven to melt butter.
4. Place about 3 chicken legs at a time in paper bag with flour mixture; shake to coat well; remove, and arrange in one of pans. Repeat until 12 chicken legs are in each pan.
5. Bake two pans of chicken, uncovered, on two racks in oven 30 minutes. Then turn legs, reverse position of pans, and bake chicken 15 minutes longer, or until fork-tender and golden brown.
6. Serve hot (or cold), heaped in half of a large skillet or platter, with Chive-Buttered Corn on the Cob in other half *as pictured*. Makes 8 to 10 servings.

DILLED PEAS WITH ARTICHOKE HEARTS

1 15-ounce can artichoke hearts	½ teaspoon salt
	¼ cup butter or margarine, melted
Ground dill seeds	
2 10-ounce packages frozen, or 2 1-pound 1-ounce cans, peas	

Day before, if desired, or early on day:
Empty can of artichoke hearts with their liquid into small bowl; stir ½ teaspoon ground dill seeds into liquid. Refrigerate several hours or overnight.
About 15 minutes before serving:
1. Cook frozen peas as package labels direct (or heat canned peas), adding ½ teaspoon ground dill seeds.
2. Meanwhile, drain liquid from artichoke hearts.
3. When peas are done, pour their hot liquid over artichoke hearts; let stand 1 minute.
4. Now drain artichoke hearts. In heated serving dish, lightly toss them with hot peas, salt, ½ teaspoon ground dill seeds, and melted butter. Serve at once *as pictured*. Makes 8 to 10 servings.

CHIVE-BUTTERED CORN ON THE COB

16 ears garden-fresh corn	Snipped chives
1 cup butter or margarine	

Just before serving:
1. Husk enough corn for first round (8 ears); remove silk; break into 2- or 3-inch pieces. Drop into plenty of rapidly boiling salted water. Bring to boil again; then boil, covered, just 3 to 5 minutes.
2. Immediately drain corn; brush with ½ cup melted butter; sprinkle with chives.
3. Heap in half of large skillet, with chicken in other half *as pictured*. (Cook second round of corn while first round is being eaten, using remaining melted butter.) Makes 8 to 10 servings.

SOUR-CREAM SLAW

1 large head crisp green cabbage	½ teaspoon granulated sugar
Minced onion	3 teaspoons salt
⅔ cup diced celery	2 tablespoons tarragon vinegar
⅔ cup slivered green pepper	Fresh or canned pineapple spears
⅔ cup coarsely-grated carrots	Large stuffed olives
½ cup sliced radishes	Large ripe olives
1 cup commercial sour cream	

Early on day, if desired:
1. Remove several shapely leaves from cabbage head and refrigerate. Prepare enough finely shredded cabbage to measure 8 cups.
2. In large bowl combine shredded cabbage, 2 tablespoons minced onion, celery, green pepper, carrots, and radishes; refrigerate.
3. In small bowl combine sour cream, 2 teaspoons minced onion, sugar, salt, and vinegar; cover; refrigerate until needed.
Just before serving:
1. Pour sour-cream dressing over vegetable mixture; toss lightly until vegetables are well coated with dressing.
2. Line a large salad bowl with cabbage leaves. Heap slaw in center; garnish with pineapple spears, stuffed and ripe olives *as pictured*. Makes 8 to 10 servings.

New-Look Buffet Supper

NEIGHBORS ALL
*Rolled Turkey Roast**
*Della Robbia Fruit Salad Wreath**
Basket of Hot Breads:
Cornsticks, Gingerbread Squares, Toasted Seeded
*English Muffins, and Curried-Mushroom Fan-Tans**
*Café Brûlot** *Fruits and Nuts*

ROLLED TURKEY ROAST

4- to 6-pound frozen	*Pepper*
boneless turkey roast	*Poultry seasoning*
Salt	*1 cup water*

About 4 hours and 30 minutes before serving:
1. Start heating oven to 350°F.
2. Unwrap frozen roast; sprinkle with salt, pepper, and poultry seasoning. Place, skin side up, on rack in small roasting pan. Add water; cover or wrap well in foil, then start roasting.
3. After about 1½ hours of roasting, remove foil and insert roast-meat thermometer into center of roast, from top down. Cover or wrap again, then return to oven until thermometer registers 180°F.—about 2½ hours longer. (If roast is not brown enough, uncover during last 15 minutes.)
4. Let roast stand 15 minutes before removing cords and arranging on platter for serving. Meanwhile, if desired, make gravy from drippings in pan. Makes about 14 servings.

DELLA ROBBIA FRUIT SALAD WREATH

½ pound red grapes	*1½ teaspoons grated*
½ pound green grapes	*orange peel*
1 egg white, slightly	*2 3-ounce packages cream*
beaten	*cheese*
Granulated sugar	*½ cup finely-chopped*
1 1-pound 14-ounce can	*pecans*
pear halves (8)	*48 large pecan halves*
1 1-pound 14-ounce can	*1 5-ounce jar process*
apricot halves (16)	*cheese spread*
1 1-pound 4-ounce can	*Curly endive*
pineapple slices (8)	*Water cress*
1 1-pound jar spiced crab	*Spicy French dressing*
apples (8)	*(optional)*
1 8-ounce package creamed	*Boston lettuce cups*
cottage cheese (1 cup)	*2 grapefruits, sectioned*
½ cup finely-snipped dates	*2 large oranges, sectioned*
¼ teaspoon almond extract	

Day before, if desired:
1. Frost grapes by dripping tiny bunchlets into slightly beaten egg white; set on cookie sheet; sprinkle with sugar; refrigerate.
2. Drain pears, apricots, pineapple, and crab apples; refrigerate.

3. Combine cottage cheese with dates, almond extract, and orange peel; refrigerate.
4. Mix cream cheese with chopped pecans; refrigerate.
5. Fill each pair of pecan halves with process cheese spread to form nut shape; refrigerate.
About 1 hour before serving:
1. Assemble fruit wreath as follows: On round 16-inch serving plate or tray, arrange bed of curly endive and water cress, with small bowl of French dressing in center, if desired. Around bowl arrange lettuce cups; fill with grapefruit sections; top with crab apples.
2. Next, in circle around lettuce cups, arrange pears, cut side up. Tuck an orange section under each; top pears with cottage-cheese mixture.
3. Now place pineapple slices in circle in between pear halves. Top each with an apricot half, cut side up. Next spoon a rounded spoonful of cream-cheese mixture into apricot halves; top with an apricot half, rounded side up.
4. Tuck grape bunchlets around edge near pineapple slices. Arrange filled pecans between pear halves and lettuce cups. Stand up water cress spriglets, tree-like, here and there. Refrigerate until served. Makes 8 servings.

CURRIED-MUSHROOM FAN-TANS

2 4-ounce cans sliced	*¾ teaspoon curry powder*
mushrooms	*12 fan-tan rolls*
½ cup soft butter or	
margarine	

Day before:
1. Combine mushrooms, drained and coarsely chopped, with butter and curry powder. Open sections of rolls; spread sections and tops with mushroom-butter mixture.
2. Wrap fan-tans, side by side, in foil; refrigerate.
About 30 minutes before serving:
1. Start heating oven to 375°F.
2. Pull down foil and away from sides of fan-tans.
3. Bake 15 minutes, or until hot and crisp. Makes 12.

CAFÉ BRÛLOT

1 orange	*1 cup brandy*
Whole cloves	*¼ cup Cointreau*
1 3-inch stick cinnamon	*1 teaspoon vanilla extract*
1 piece lemon peel, 3	*1 quart very hot, strong*
inches long	*black coffee*
6 lumps sugar	

Just before serving:
1. From orange, cut a continuous strip of orange peel, 1 inch wide; then stick it with cloves at 1-inch intervals.
2. Place orange peel in silver punch bowl or large chafing dish with cinnamon, lemon peel, and sugar.

Café Brûlot

Imperial Pears

Cranberry Pudding Mold

Max's Super Cheese Pie

At serving time:

1.   In an attractive small saucepan heat brandy over *low* heat so that it does not catch fire. Meanwhile, pour Cointreau and vanilla into punch bowl; then pour in coffee (it must be hot, hot, hot).

2.   Immediately carry punch bowl and brandy to table in darkened room. Fill ladle with hot brandy; pour rest over coffee in bowl. Give one of guests the honor of lighting brandy in ladle with long match. Then, slowly pour flaming brandy into coffee in bowl *as pictured on page 25.* Serve in demitasse, brûlot, or diable cups. Makes 8 servings.

BUFFET WITHOUT BOTHER
*Bite-Size Olive Crescents**
California Casserole with Butter Crumb Dumplings**
Broccoli with Lemon Butter
Tossed Salad with Oil and Vinegar Dressing
*Mocha Cream Torte**
Coffee or Tea

BITE-SIZE OLIVE CRESCENTS

1 package refrigerated crescent rolls	Pitted ripe olives, stuffed with almond slivers

1.   Start heating oven to 375°F.
2.   Unroll refrigerated rolls; separate dough into 8 triangles; cut each into 3 small triangles. Place an olive on each triangle; roll up into crescents.
3.   Bake 10 to 12 minutes, or until golden. Makes 24.

CALIFORNIA CASSEROLE

2 pounds veal round steak	2 10½-ounce cans condensed cream-of-chicken soup, undiluted
⅓ cup regular all-purpose flour	
1 teaspoon paprika	1 15-ounce can onions
¼ cup salad oil	Butter Crumb Dumplings, below
½ teaspoon salt	
⅛ teaspoon pepper	1 cup commercial sour cream
1 cup water	

About 1 hour and 30 minutes before serving:

1.   Cut veal into 2-inch pieces; coat with flour mixed with paprika. Brown in hot oil in skillet. Add salt, pepper, and water; simmer, covered, 30 minutes, or until tender. Transfer to 3-quart casserole.
2.   Start heating oven to 425°F.
3.   In same skillet, heat 1 can chicken soup. Drain onions, reserving liquid. Add onion liquid plus enough water to measure 1½ cups to soup; bring to boil; pour over meat. Toss in onions; top with dumplings.
4.   Bake, uncovered, 25 to 30 minutes. Serve, topped with sauce made by heating 1 can chicken soup with sour cream just until hot. Makes 8 to 10 servings.
BUTTER CREAM DUMPLINGS: Sift 2 cups sifted reg-

ular all-purpose flour with 4 teaspoons double-acting baking powder, ½ teaspoon salt, and 1 teaspoon poultry seasoning. Add 1 teaspoon celery seed, 1 teaspoon instant minced onion, and 1 teaspoon poppy seed (optional). Stir in ¼ cup salad oil and 1 cup milk until a moist dough. Drop, a rounded tablespoon at a time, in ¼ cup melted butter or margarine, then roll in 1 cup packaged dried bread crumbs to coat. Makes 16 to 18.

MOCHA CREAM TORTE

1 package white-cake mix	1½ teaspoons instant coffee powder
2 cups heavy cream	
1 package butter-cream milk-chocolate-frosting mix	2 crushed toffee candy bars

Early on day:

1.   Prepare and bake cake mix in 2 8- or 9-inch layer-cake pans as package label directs; cool completely.
2.   Beat heavy cream with frosting mix and instant coffee powder until thickened. Use half of it to fill center and frost top of one cake layer, split in half horizontally. Garnish with 1 crushed candy bar. Repeat with second layer. Refrigerate.
3.   To serve, cut each two-layer torte into 8 wedges; arrange on tray. Makes 16 servings.

THE MORE THE MERRIER
*Curried-Rice Meat-Ball Casserole**
All Romaine Salad
*Seeded Corn Crisps**
*Cranberry Pudding Mold**
Hot Coffee

CURRIED-RICE MEAT-BALL CASSEROLE

1½ pounds small white onions	⅓ to ½ cup salad oil
	1½ pounds small fresh mushrooms
1 bunch small carrots, halved crosswise	
1 10-ounce package frozen peas, thawed	1 10½-ounce can condensed cream-of-mushroom soup, undiluted
2 pounds chuck, ground	¾ teaspoon nutmeg
1 egg	¾ teaspoon bottled sauce for gravy
1 cup day-old bread crumbs	
¾ teaspoon marjoram	¾ teaspoon onion salt or monosodium glutamate
2½ teaspoons salt	
¾ teaspoon Worcestershire	3 cups hot cooked rice
⅔ cup milk	1 teaspoon curry powder

About 1 hour and 30 minutes before serving:

1.   In large saucepan heat 1 inch salted water to boiling; add onions and carrots; cook, covered, 20 minutes, or until barely tender-crisp; top with thawed peas; cover; turn off heat.

2. Meanwhile, with fork, lightly mix chuck with egg, bread crumbs, marjoram, salt, Worcestershire, and milk. Drop by tablespoonfuls into hot oil in skillet; brown quickly on both sides; remove.

3. Start heating oven to 400°F.

4. In same skillet, sauté mushrooms until tender—about 5 minutes; remove. Then in same skillet, heat soup with nutmeg, bottled sauce for gravy, and onion salt. Arrange drained peas, carrots, onions, mushrooms, and meat balls in 3-quart casserole. Pour in soup.

5. Bake, uncovered, 25 minutes. Meanwhile, cook rice, then toss it with curry and arrange around top edge of casserole *as pictured on page 15.* Bake 10 minutes longer, or until bubbly. Makes 8 servings.

SEEDED CORN CRISPS

1 cup yellow corn meal	2 tablespoons melted
½ cup sifted regular all-	shortening
purpose flour	⅓ cup milk
½ teaspoon salt	½ teaspoon poppy seeds
¼ teaspoon baking soda	

Make several days ahead, or early on day:

1. Start heating oven to 350°F.

2. Sift corn meal with flour, salt, and baking soda; stir in shortening, milk, and poppy seeds.

3. On lightly floured surface, knead dough 6 to 8 times, or until it just holds together. Break off nickel-size pieces; with rolling pin, roll each into a very thin, 4-inch round, leaving edges ragged.

4. Bake on ungreased cookie sheet, 15 minutes, or until golden.

Just before serving:
Brush crisps with melted butter or margarine; sprinkle with salt. Makes 24.

CRANBERRY PUDDING MOLD

½ cup butter or margarine	⅛ teaspoon salt
1 cup granulated sugar	¾ cup milk
2 eggs, unbeaten	3 tablespoons cake flour
2¾ cups sifted cake flour	1½ cups whole cranberries
3½ teaspoons double-acting	Boiling water
baking powder	Hard sauce or light cream

About 2 hours before serving:

1. Thoroughly grease and flour a 1½-quart tube mold and its cover.

2. In large bowl, with mixer at medium speed, beat butter until creamy. Gradually add sugar, beating mixture until light and fluffy. Then add eggs; beat well.

3. Sift 2¾ cups flour with baking powder and salt. Now, with mixer at low speed, alternately beat flour and milk into butter mixture, starting and ending with flour.

4. Onto wax paper, sprinkle 3 tablespoons cake flour;

in it roll cranberries until coated. Fold cranberries into batter, then turn into mold and cover.

5. Place pudding on trivet in deep kettle. Add enough boiling water to come halfway up its sides. Steam, covered, 1 hour and 10 minutes, or until done, replenishing boiling water if necessary to keep it at its original level.

6. When done, remove mold to wire rack; remove cover and let stand 30 minutes. Then, with long spatula, carefully loosen pudding from sides, then from center of mold. Invert on serving dish; lift off mold.

7. In serving, cut pudding into fourths, lengthwise; then with pie server, lift each wedge to waiting plate and cut into 3 crosswise servings. Serve with hard sauce *as pictured on page 26.* Makes 12 servings.

To do ahead: Make pudding several days ahead. After steaming it, remove from mold as in step 6 above. Cool, then wrap pudding in foil and refrigerate until needed. To serve, heat foil-wrapped pudding in 325°F. oven 45 minutes, or until hot.

SIT-DOWN-IN-STYLE BUFFET
Chilled Curried Vichysoisse (from frozen potato soup)
Roast Beef with Green Peas
Tuna-Stuffed Tomatoes
Waldorf Salad Bowl
Max's Super Cheese Pie* with Strawberry Crown
Coffee   Assorted Chocolates

MAX'S SUPER CHEESE PIE

1⅓ cups packaged	2 eggs
graham-cracker crumbs	½ cup granulated sugar
⅓ cup brown sugar	½ teaspoon vanilla extract
½ teaspoon cinnamon	1 cup commercial sour
⅓ cup melted butter or	cream
margarine	12 strawberries
1½ 8-ounce packages	
cream cheese	

About 4 hours before serving:

1. In a well-greased 9-inch pie plate, mix graham-cracker crumbs, brown sugar, cinnamon, and melted butter until crumbly. With back of spoon press to bottom and sides of pie plate. Refrigerate until needed.

2. Start heating oven to 350°F.

3. In small bowl beat together cream cheese, eggs, granulated sugar, and vanilla until smooth and creamy. Turn this mixture into crumb crust.

4. Bake 35 minutes, or until firm. Then spread sour cream on top and allow pie to cool.

5. Top cooled pie with Strawberry Crown: Hull strawberries, quarter them lengthwise, then cut off hulled end, if necessary, to make quarters of fairly equal length. Surround edge of pie with these strawberry quarters, leaning slantwise with hulled ends down *as pictured on page 26.* Makes 10 servings.

To be perfect, company dinners should be easy on the host and hostess and a pleasure to the guests. Rigid serving rules are no more. The key today is *convenience*—any way that works gracefully for you and deliciously for your guests. §Some strategy is necessary for a successful company dinner. Host and hostess should prearrange their routine—who is to serve what—

Perfect Company Dinners

so there is no last-minute foul-up. Start by keeping the menu manageable. Save yourself by serving the first course in the living room. While guests sip and/or dip, you can put the salad and main courses on the table. Or place the first course (a glass of juice or mug of soup) to right of each water glass to be sipped with the main course. § Serve all-in-one main dishes whenever possible. Do your cooking in serving dishes pretty enough to come right to the table. Set salad plates and bowl at hostess' place for her to serve while host carves, and serves vegetables. Or place individual salads to left of each place setting. In lieu of salads, pass a platter of crisp raw relishes with the main course. Prebutter hot breads. Then let salad plates double as bread-and-butter plates. § The host and hostess share the responsibility of keeping the conversation going. If the hostess is busy removing dinner plates and serving dessert, this duty is up to the host. After clearing the main course, the hostess places the dessert in front of each guest, from the left. Or she may serve the dessert on plates from her place at the table. A hostess cart is handy for this, and also for the coffee service. If preferred, place the cart at host's place for serving the vegetables.

TO SET AN INVITING TABLE

Silver, china, and glasses are usually arranged in a definite order. Feel free, though, to change it as you need or wish, as long as the effect is charming. Set the table well ahead. Place mats are perfectly proper, but if you prefer a cloth, choose an easy-to-launder one of white, cream, or pastel. A damask cloth should be laid over a table pad. Let the cloth extend over edge of table 12 to 15 inches. A sheer embroidered or lace cloth goes directly on the table with an overhang of 15 to 18 inches. Napkins can match or contrast with the cloth or mats. Dinner napkins should be large—18-inches or more square. Fold them in an oblong with open corner at right. Place on plate in center of each place if dinner is formal, or to left of forks. §*Setting silver*. Place no more than three pieces of silver on each side of plate. Try to allow 20 to 24 inches for each place. Space equidistantly and as far apart as table will allow. Lay silver 1 inch in from edge of table or mat, in a straight line, and in the order used. All forks go at left of plate. If salad goes with main course, put salad fork to right of dinner fork; if salad is first course, put it to left of dinner fork (or eliminate it altogether and let guests use dinner fork for both salad and main course). Knife should be placed at right of plate, cutting edge toward plate. Next, at right, place fruit and/or soup spoon, bowl up. Dessert silver may be placed as follows, or may be placed on plate when dessert is served: If fork, place to right of salad fork; if spoon, place to right of knife. (Coffee, tea, or demitasse spoons always go on the saucer parallel to the handle of the cup.) §*Glassware and china*. Goblet or water glass is placed at the tip of the knife. If wine is to be served, wine glass goes to right of water glass. Bread-and-butter plate goes at tip of fork, with butter spreader in place. A 10-inch service plate is always used at formal dinners, and is placed in center of each place, 1 inch in from edge of table. It is removed just before the main course. Salad plates should be put in place just before dinner is announced. §*Incidentals*. Place chairs with edge just under cloth. Salt should be within reach of every four guests. Set gravy, relishes, and bread on table if there is space, with serving silver beside them, to be passed by guests. Fill water glasses three-fourths full just before dinner is announced. Have a pitcher of water nearby for refilling glasses between courses.

WHO SITS WHERE

As guests enter the dining room, the hostess tells each one where to sit. (Plan your arrangement ahead.) Usually the host sits at one end of the table, hostess at the other. To host's immediate right is lady guest of honor, with female guest of next importance at his left. To hostess' immediate right is gentleman guest of honor, with male guest of next importance to her left.

TO SERVE GUESTS

Place main dish or platter and vegetable dishes on hot pads in front of host, with carving knife and fork and serving silver. Pile of heated plates should go to his left with one in front of him. If the person to the host's left is to serve the vegetables, the host puts a portion of the main dish on a plate, then passes it along for serving of vegetables. The filled plate then goes to the guest being served. Some hosts prefer to serve the hostess first, then progress to her right around the table. Others would rather begin with the female guest of honor, then to the right around the table, with host last.

MOST ORIGINAL
Beef Stroganoff à la Palmer*
Saffron Rice with Olives*
French-Style Green Beans with Almond Slivers
Tossed Greens with Grated Parmesan Cheese
Chilled Orange, Grapefruit, and Grapes
(with grated coconut and confectioners' sugar)
Coffee

BEEF STROGANOFF À LA PALMER

1 pint commercial sour cream	¼ pound butter or margarine
1 envelope onion-soup mix	⅛ teaspoon olive oil
4 pounds boned beef chuck, 1¼ to 1½ inches thick	½ to ¾ cup cut-up scallions
Unseasoned instant meat tenderizer	½ cup dry sherry
	Water cress or parsley

Day before:
Mix sour cream with onion-soup mix; refrigerate.
Early on day:
1.   Treat boned chuck with meat tenderizer exactly as label directs; refrigerate 1 hour.
2.   Now slice meat paper thin, cutting diagonally across grain; wrap, then refrigerate.
About 1 hour before serving:
1.   In large skillet, melt butter with olive oil; in it sauté scallions until browned. Stir into sour cream mixture.
2.   Now lay beef slices, side by side, in hot skillet until bottom is covered. Then, starting with the first slice laid in pan, and going on to the next, turn each one over and brown other side (it takes about ½ minute for each side). Then remove beef, slice by slice, to heated platter, overlapping slices; keep warm. Repeat until all meat is brown.
3.   Allow skillet to cool, then place it over low heat and add sherry. As sherry warms, scrape bits of meat from bottom of skillet. When mixture simmers, pour any juices from meat platter into sour-cream mixture; then stir it into wine in skillet. When this sauce is just hot (don't let it boil), pour it over beef slices; serve immediately, garnished with water cress. Makes 8 servings.

SAFFRON RICE WITH OLIVES

1 cup raw regular or processed white rice	2 chicken-bouillon cubes
2 tablespoons butter or margarine	½ teaspoon saffron
2 cups water	1 3-ounce jar small pimento-stuffed olives

About 45 minutes before serving:
1.   Start heating oven to 350°F.
2.   Place rice and butter in greased 1½-quart casserole.

In saucepan bring water to boil; add bouillon cubes and saffron; stir until dissolved. Pour this mixture into casserole.
3.   Bake, covered, 30 minutes.
4.   When saffron-rice mixture is baked, with 2-tined fork, stir in olives, drained and halved crosswise. Makes 8 servings.

BACHELOR DINNER
Steak Sublime*
Boiled New Potatoes
French-Style Green Beans with Toasted Almonds
Piquant Artichoke-Heart Salad*
Cheesecake   Coffee

STEAK SUBLIME

1 porterhouse steak, 2 inches thick	4 shallots, finely chopped, or 1 tablespoon instant minced onion
Seasoned salt	
Seasoned pepper	1 tablespoon snipped parsley
¼ pound fresh mushrooms, halved	1 teaspoon lemon juice
¼ cup butter or margarine	¼ teaspoon salt
½ cup red wine	

About 40 minutes before serving:
1.   Preheat broiler 10 minutes, or as manufacturer directs. Sprinkle steak on both sides with seasoned salt and pepper.
2.   Broil steak 10 to 15 minutes on each side for rare, or longer, if desired.
3.   Meanwhile, in large skillet, sauté mushrooms in butter until golden; add wine, shallots, parsley, lemon juice, salt, and dash seasoned pepper. Bring to boil; then simmer 5 minutes. Keep sauce warm until steak is done.
4.   Serve steak on warm platter, with mushrooms and wine sauce over it. Makes 3 or 4 servings.

PIQUANT ARTICHOKE-HEART SALAD

1 9-ounce package frozen artichoke hearts	¼ cup wine vinegar
1 envelope garlic-salad-dressing mix	2 tablespoons sherry
	Boston lettuce

Early on day, or several hours before serving:
1.   Cook artichokes as package label directs; drain.
2.   Prepare salad dressing from mix as label directs, but use wine vinegar, and substitute sherry for water. Place artichokes in small bowl; pour half of dressing over them; cover; refrigerate at least 2 hours. Refrigerate rest of dressing.
3.   At serving time arrange lettuce on salad plates; spoon artichokes with their dressing on lettuce. Pass extra dressing, if desired. Makes 4 generous servings.

DINNER ON THE TERRACE
Avocado Madrilène*
Grecian Beef with Cheese Noodles*
Buttered Broccoli
Tossed Salad
Lemon-Chiffon Tarts
Iced Coffee

AVOCADO MADRILÈNE

Madrilène, below, or 1
  12½-ounce can
  madrilène
Cracked ice

3 ripe avocados
1 tablespoon lemon juice
Lime and lemon wedges

Day before:
Make Madrilène; refrigerate (or refrigerate canned madrilène).
About 10 minutes before serving:
1.   Arrange layer of ice in deep serving tray; refrigerate.
2.   Cut avocados in half lengthwise; remove pits. Brush cut surfaces with lemon juice, then arrange halves on ice *as pictured on page 32.*
3.   With fork, break up madrilène; then use to fill avocado halves. In center of tray arrange lemon and lime wedges. Serve as first course. Makes 6 servings.

MADRILÈNE

1 cup canned tomato juice
1 cup canned chicken
  broth
10 celery leaves
1 lemon slice
⅛ teaspoon thyme
½ cup cold water

1 envelope unflavored
  gelatin
1 teaspoon bitters
½ teaspoon salt
¼ teaspoon onion salt
⅛ teaspoon pepper
Red food color

1.   In saucepan combine tomato juice, chicken broth, celery leaves, lemon slice, thyme, and ¼ cup water. Simmer 10 minutes, then strain into bowl.
2.   Meanwhile, onto ¼ cup water, sprinkle gelatin; stir into hot tomato-juice mixture until dissolved. Then stir in bitters, salt, onion salt, pepper, and a few drops food color. Refrigerate.

GRECIAN BEEF WITH CHEESE NOODLES

1½ pounds chuck steak,
  boned and trimmed of fat
Instant meat tenderizer
¼ cup salad oil
2 medium onions, sliced
3 tablespoons regular all-
  purpose flour
1 10½-ounce can con-
  densed tomato soup,
  undiluted

1 cup water
2 tablespoons lemon juice
⅛ teaspoon ground cloves
¼ teaspoon cinnamon
½ teaspoon salt
¼ teaspoon pepper
3 cups uncooked noodles
½ cup grated Parmesan
  cheese

About 1 hour and 20 minutes before serving:
1.   Treat chuck with meat tenderizer as label directs; cut into thin bite-size pieces, about 1½ by ¼ inch.
2.   In hot oil, in skillet, brown meat pieces; then remove meat. In same skillet sauté onion slices until golden. Stir in flour, then soup and water.
3.   Return meat to skillet; add lemon juice, cloves, cinnamon, salt, and pepper. Simmer, covered, about 45 minutes, or until meat is fork-tender.
4.   Just before meat is done, cook noodles as package label directs; then mix in grated cheese. On heated platter, serve meat over noodles. Makes 4 to 6 servings.

FIT FOR A KING
Short Rib Crown Roast* with Herb-Potato Stuffing*
Browned Baby Onions
Orange Slices on Water Cress
Hot Rolls
Slipped Custard Pie   Coffee

SHORT RIB CROWN ROAST

2 sections short ribs, 4
  inches high (about 10
  ribs)
Seasoned instant meat
  tenderizer
Onion salt
Garlic salt

Herb-Potato Stuffing,
  page 33
3 pounds small white
  onions
¼ cup currant jelly,
  melted

About 3 hours before serving:
1.   Have meatman tie and "sew" 2 sections of short ribs together in a crown, with bone sides out. Treat ribs with meat tenderizer as label directs; then sprinkle with onion and garlic salts. Place in shallow roasting pan.
2.   Make Herb-Potato Stuffing; heap in crown; cover with "cap" of foil.
3.   Start heating oven to 350°F.
4.   Insert roast-meat thermometer, with its tip at center of thickest meaty section of one of ribs.
5.   Roast about 2 hours, or until meat thermometer registers 150°F. for medium-rare, or to desired doneness.
6.   Meanwhile, cook onions in boiling salted water to cover until almost tender; drain.

Avocado Madrilène

Short Rib Crown Roast

Company Hungarian Roast

7. When roast is done, remove foil; spoon some of drippings from pan over stuffing; brush all meat surfaces with melted jelly. Return to 400°F. oven for 10 minutes to glaze roast and brown stuffing.

8. Remove roast to serving platter; let stand about 20 minutes before serving.

9. Meanwhile, lay onions in meat drippings in roasting pan; brown in 400°F. oven about 15 minutes. Arrange onions around roast *as pictured opposite*. Makes about 10 servings.

HERB-POTATO STUFFING

1 medium onion, minced	1 medium carrot, coarsely
2 tablespoons shortening	grated
1 cup diced celery	½ cup snipped parsley
3 cups cooked, drained,	¼ teaspoon sage
packaged hash-browned	½ teaspoon salt
potatoes	⅛ teaspoon pepper
¼ cup packaged dried	1 egg, beaten
bread crumbs	

In large skillet, sauté onion, in shortening until golden; add celery and cook until tender; add potatoes, bread crumbs, carrot, parsley, sage, salt, pepper, and egg. Mix well, then heap in center of Short Rib Crown Roast.

FRANKLY IMPRESSIVE
Company Hungarian Roast*
Baked Potatoes   Peas and Carrots
Green Salad
Hot Butterflake Rolls
Sunny Hill Apple Pie*   *Coffee*

COMPANY HUNGARIAN ROAST

6 pounds lean sirloin	3 10-ounce packages frozen
roast, in one piece	peas with carrots
1½ teaspoons salt	Butter or margarine
¼ teaspoon pepper	1 teaspoon regular all-
Paprika	purpose flour
¾ pound ready-to-eat	1 cup commercial sour
Canadian-style bacon	cream
slices	¼ cup white wine
2 8-ounce packages natural	¼ cup water
Swiss-cheese slices	1 teaspoon seasoned salt
¼ cup salad oil	1 small onion
10 medium baking potatoes	Water cress

Early on day:

1. Cut roast crosswise, to a depth of about 1 inch from bottom, into 10 slices. Sprinkle roast top and slices, with 1 teaspoon salt, pepper, and ½ teaspoon paprika. In each cut place 3 bacon slices, side by side, then 1 slice Swiss cheese, trimmed at top corners.

2. Now tie roast lengthwise securely. Set on rack in shallow roasting pan; refrigerate.

About 2 hours and 15 minutes before serving:

1. Start heating oven to 450°F.

2. In small saucepan heat salad oil; pour over top and sides of meat.

3. Roast sirloin 30 minutes, then arrange potatoes around roasting pan on oven rack.

4. Roast 30 minutes, basting sirloin occasionally; then cover with foil and roast 45 minutes longer for very rare, or about 65 minutes longer for medium rare.

5. Meanwhile, in medium saucepan cook peas with carrots as package label directs; drain; add 3 tablespoons butter; keep warm.

6. When done, remove roast from oven to large serving platter; remove strings. Pour all but 2 tablespoons fat from roasting pan. Scrape pan well; then, over medium heat, add flour, sour cream, wine, water, ½ teaspoon salt, and seasoned salt, stirring until smooth. Strain into gravy dish.

7. Remove potatoes from oven; in top of each cut a lengthwise slit; insert a pat of butter, then sprinkle with paprika. Arrange them and carrot-pea mixture alongside of roast, or in serving dishes. Garnish with onion rings and water cress. Makes about 10 servings.

SUNNY HILL APPLE PIE

1 package piecrust mix	¼ teaspoon cinnamon
7 medium apples	6 tablespoons granulated
2 tablespoons dark seed-	sugar
less raisins	3 eggs
2 tablespoons regular all-	2 tablespoons slivered
purpose flour	almonds
1 cup light cream	¼ cup apricot preserves

Early on day:

1. Prepare piecrust as package label directs; use to line 11-inch pie plate, making fluted or rope edge; prick bottom well with fork.

2. Start heating oven to 375°F.

3. Wash, pare, and core apples; cut 1-inch-thick slice from one side of each; then, on other side of each, cut crisscross pattern ½ inch deep. In lined pie plate, arrange 6 apples, crisscross side up, in circle; center seventh one.

4. Bake 30 minutes.

5. While pie bakes, soak raisins in hot water to cover. Also, in bowl, combine flour, cream, cinnamon, and sugar, stirring until smooth. Blend in eggs, one at a time. Pour this custard around apples.

6. Bake 35 minutes, or until almost set.

7. Drain raisins; sprinkle over custard with almonds. Bake 15 minutes longer, or until golden. Remove from oven to wire rack.

8. Heat apricot preserves with 2 teaspoons water, stirring until smooth. Brush over apples. Cool, then serve in wedges. Makes about 10 servings.

SUPER-EDIBLE COMBINATION
*Three-Tastes Roast**
*Pommes de Terre Anna**   Green Peas with Scallions
Raw Vegetable Relish Tray   Hot Rolls
Chocolate-Mint Parfaits   Coffee

THREE-TASTES ROAST

1½ pounds round steak, ¼ inch
    thick
1½ pounds fresh ham steak, ¼ inch
    thick
1½ pounds veal steak, ¼ inch
    thick
Salt
Pepper

½ cup snipped parsley
2 tablespoons shortening
1 10½-ounce can condensed
    consommé, undiluted
½ cup sliced celery
1 medium onion, sliced
4 whole cloves
¼ cup regular all-purpose flour

About 3 hours before serving:

1. Sprinkle round, ham, and veal steaks with salt and pepper, then generously with snipped parsley. Stack steaks, one on the other, starting with round and ending with veal. Roll up steaks, jelly-roll fashion; with cord, tie gently across, then lengthwise, to keep shape.
2. Start heating oven to 325°F.
3. In Dutch oven, over medium heat, heat shortening; in it brown meat roll on all sides. Pour in consommé; add celery, onion, and cloves.
4. Roast, covered, 2½ hours, or until tender.
5. Remove meat, then cords. Strain gravy; blend flour with ¼ cup water; stir into gravy. Then cook, over medium heat, stirring until thickened.
6. Serve meat hot, in slices, with gravy *as pictured*. Makes 8 to 10 servings.

POMMES DE TERRE ANNA

2 pounds medium white potatoes
4 tablespoons butter or margarine

1½ teaspoons salt
¼ teaspoon pepper

About 1 hour and 30 minutes before serving:

1. Wash, then parboil potatoes by cooking them, in boiling water to cover, 10 minutes. Drain, peel, then slice potatoes ⅛ inch thick.
2. Start heating oven to 425°F.
3. Butter a 1-quart baking dish with 1 tablespoon butter. Starting at center bottom of dish, line bottom and sides with slightly overlapping potato slices. Sprinkle with ½ teaspoon salt and ⅛ teaspoon pepper; dot with 1 tablespoon butter.
4. Over this layer arrange half of remaining potato slices; sprinkle with ½ teaspoon salt and ⅛ teaspoon pepper; dot with 1 tablespoon butter. Cover with rest of potatoes; add rest of salt and butter.
5. Bake about 1 hour, or until golden.
6. To serve, loosen potatoes around edges; invert serving dish on top, then unmold and cut into wedges *as pictured*. Makes 6 servings.
INSTANT POMMES DE TERRE ANNA: Boil, then drain 1 package instant pre-sliced frying potatoes as label directs. Then, in 1-quart baking dish, layer them with 4 tablespoons butter as above, omitting salt and pepper and sprinkling with contents of herb-spice packet which comes in package. Bake at 425°F. 50 minutes, or until golden.

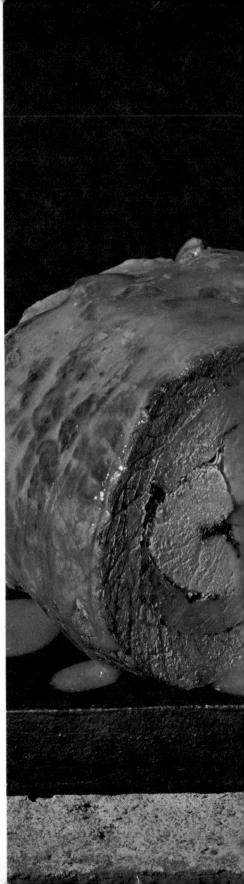

Three-Tastes Roast, Pommes de Terre Anna

HANDSOME AND HEARTY
Three-Layer Beef-and-Vegetable Loaf*
Pickle Coleslaw
Rye-Bread Slices
Coffee-Cognac Ice Cream   *Coffee*

THREE-LAYER
BEEF-AND-VEGETABLE LOAF

2 cups cooked carrot slices (about ¾ pound)	1 pound chuck, ground
2 eggs	¼ cup milk
¼ cup milk	1 tablespoon prepared horse-radish
½ teaspoon salt	1½ teaspoons salt
Dash nutmeg	1 teaspoon prepared mustard
2 cups seasoned mashed potatoes	¼ cup catchup
¼ cup shredded Parmesan cheese	¼ cup minced onion
2 eggs	1 cup drained cooked or canned peas

About 2 hours before serving:
1. Grease well 10-by-5-by-3-inch loaf pan. In bottom of pan arrange carrot slices. In small bowl beat 2 eggs until frothy; stir in ¼ cup milk, ½ teaspoon salt, and nutmeg. Pour this custard over carrots.
2. To mashed potatoes add cheese; lightly spread on top of carrot layer.
3. Start heating oven to 400°F.
4. In medium bowl beat 2 eggs slightly; then add chuck, ¼ cup milk, horse-radish, 1½ teaspoons salt, mustard, catchup, onion and drained peas. Spread chuck mixture lightly, in a layer, over mashed potatoes.
5. Bake 50 minutes, with sheet of foil, slightly larger than loaf pan, on rack beneath to catch any drippings.
6. Let loaf stand at room temperature 30 minutes, then invert on serving platter. Slice and serve *as pictured on page 39.* Makes 8 servings.

YOUNG AT HEART
Veal Inverness*
Parsleyed Carrots and Potatoes*
Boiled Onions with Paprika
Spinach Salad Bowl
Hot Seeded Bread Sticks*
Snow Pudding   *Coffee*

VEAL INVERNESS

1 or 2 cloves garlic, mashed (optional)	¼ teaspoon pepper
⅓ cup salad oil	2 pounds veal cutlet, ¼ inch thick, or 4 veal loin chops, ¾ inch thick
3 tablespoons soy sauce	
2 tablespoons catchup	
1 tablespoon vinegar	2 tablespoons salad oil

1. For marinade, in shallow pan combine garlic, ⅓

cup salad oil, soy sauce, catchup, vinegar, and pepper.
2. Cut veal into serving pieces. Place in marinade; turn to coat well; refrigerate.
About 35 minutes before serving:
In 2 tablespoons hot oil, in skillet, over medium heat, sauté veal about 15 minutes on each side, or until nicely browned and fork-tender. Arrange on heated platter. Makes 4 servings.

PARSLEYED CARROTS AND POTATOES

2 cups scraped slivered carrots	¾ cup boiling water
2 cups pared slivered potatoes	3 tablespoons melted butter or margarine
1¼ teaspoons salt	⅛ teaspoon pepper
	½ cup snipped parsley

1. Cook carrots and potatoes with salt in boiling water, covered, 10 minutes, or until tender.
2. Drain; add butter, pepper, and parsley; toss, then serve. Or after draining, mash, then season. Makes 4 servings.

HOT SEEDED BREAD STICKS

Bread sticks	Poppy seeds
Salad oil	

Brush bread sticks with salad oil; heat in skillet over low heat, shaking skillet occasionally. Sprinkle with poppy seeds, then serve.

DAY-BEFORE COMPANY DINNER
Veal Casserole Chow Mein* on Rice Nests*
Buttered Julienne Carrots with Parsley Flakes
Lettuce and Tomato Salad, Dressing
Heavenly Salt Sticks
Snow-Capped Moist Chocolate Cake*
Coffee

VEAL CASSEROLE CHOW MEIN

2 pounds veal round, cut into ¾-inch cubes	1 cup boiling water
½ cup butter or margarine	½ teaspoon salt
½ teaspoon salt	½ cup regular all-purpose flour
⅛ teaspoon pepper	1 teaspoon monosodium glutamate
½ cup chopped onions	
½ cup coarsely-chopped green pepper	1 teaspoon celery salt
	1 quart milk, heated
2 cups celery, cut into 1-inch pieces	1 4-ounce can fried chow-mein noodles

Day before:
1. In Dutch oven, brown veal in butter until golden. Sprinkle with ½ teaspoon salt and pepper; add onions and green pepper. Cover; cook over low heat 20 to 30 minutes, or until tender.

2. Cook celery, covered, in boiling water and ½ teaspoon salt until tender (don't drain).

3. Sprinkle veal mixture with flour, monosodium glutamate, and celery salt; stir well. Add milk; cook, stirring, until thickened. Add undrained celery. Season to taste. Pour into 2-quart casserole; refrigerate.

Next day, about 40 minutes before serving:

1. Start heating oven to 425°F.

2. Bake casserole, uncovered, 15 to 20 minutes, or until bubbly; scatter noodles on top. Bake 10 minutes longer. Serve on Rice Nests. Makes 8 servings.

RICE NESTS: With hot-fluffy cooked rice and large ice-cream scoop, make 8 balls of rice. Place on heated serving plate; keep warm. At serving time place a ball of rice on each plate; with large serving spoon make a well in center, then spoon on generous serving of Veal Casserole Chow Mein.

SNOW-CAPPED MOIST CHOCOLATE CAKE

2 cups sifted regular all-purpose flour	1½ teaspoons double-acting baking powder
1 cup granulated sugar	2 eggs
½ cup Dutch-process cocoa	1 cup mayonnaise
1 teaspoon salt	1 cup water
1½ teaspoons baking soda	1½ tablespoons vanilla extract

Day before:

1. Start heating oven to 350°F. Grease and lightly flour 9-by-9-by-2-inch baking pan.

2. Into large bowl sift flour, sugar, cocoa, salt, baking soda, and baking powder; add eggs, mayonnaise, water, and vanilla. With mixer at medium speed, beat until well blended. Pour into prepared pan.

3. Bake 40 minutes, or until cake tester, inserted in center, comes out clean. Cool.

4. Frost with favorite butter-cream frosting. Cut into 12 generous squares. To store cake, wrap well in saran or foil.

HUNGRY-GUEST PLEASER

Veal Cutlets Magnifico* with Golden Potato Purée
Green Salad with Fresh Herbs   Hot Rolls
Prune Compote à la Sour Cream   Coffee

VEAL CUTLETS MAGNIFICO

3 pounds white potatoes	½ cup heavy cream
3½ teaspoons salt	1 tablespoon cognac
Boiling water	1 teaspoon seasoned salt
⅛ teaspoon pepper	1 8-ounce package Mozarella cheese
¼ cup milk	
5 tablespoons butter or margarine	1 4-ounce package Canadian-style bacon
1 egg, beaten	Few thin unpeeled cucumber slices
5 boneless veal cutlets, each ½ inch thick (about 1½ pounds)	2 medium tomatoes
½ cup cold water	1 tablespoon snipped parsley
½ cup dry white wine	

Day before:

1. Wash, pare, then quarter potatoes. Cook, with 1½ teaspoons salt in boiling water to cover, 20 minutes, or until tender; drain.

2. Mash potatoes; add 1½ teaspoons salt, pepper, milk, 2 tablespoons butter, and all but 2 tablespoons beaten egg. Beat until fluffy; set aside.

3. Cut each veal cutlet in half crosswise. Sprinkle, on both sides, with ½ teaspoon salt.

4. In large skillet heat 3 tablespoons butter. Over medium-high heat, brown cutlets on both sides, turning once. Remove cutlets from heat; transfer to center of oven-proof platter, or 19-by-9-by-2-inch glass baking dish, arranging them side by side.

5. Scrape skillet well; then, while stirring, add cold water, wine, cream, and cognac; add seasoned salt; bring to boil, stirring, then set aside.

6. Now, with mashed potatoes in decorating bag, and number 9 pastry tube in place, press potatoes out in border along edge of platter or baking dish, using circular motion, counter clockwise as shown. Then brush potatoes with 2 tablespoons reserved beaten egg.

7. Pour sauce over cutlets. Cut Mozarella into 10 ¼-inch-thick slices; place a slice on each cutlet, then top with Canadian-style bacon slice. Cover with saran; refrigerate until needed next day.

Next day, about 1 hour before serving:

1. Start heating oven to 375°F.

2. Bake veal 35 to 45 minutes, or until potatoes are golden and cutlets are fork-tender.

3. Remove from oven. Cut a slit from edge to center of each thin cucumber slice; use to decorate center of baking dish. Decorate potatoes with thin wedges of tomato and snipped parsley *as pictured on page 39.* Makes 5 or 6 servings.

TALK OF THE TOWN
Roast Leg of Lamb with Mint Sauce
*Baked Potato par Excellence**
*Broccoli Sunburst**
Hot Poppy-Seed Rolls
*Ginger Crème Pie**   Coffee*

BAKED POTATO PAR EXCELLENCE

Medium or large unpared potatoes	Toppings: Crumbled blue cheese, seasoned
Salad oil	commercial sour cream,
Salt	sliced ripe or chopped
Butter or margarine	stuffed olives, snipped
Paprika	chives, or bacon bits

1. Select potatoes of as nearly the same size as possible, so they will bake in same length of time. Wash, ten dry potatoes. Rub each with salad oil.
2. Start heating oven to 450°F.
3. Arrange potatoes on cookie sheet or oven rack. Bake 45 to 60 minutes, or until fork-tender. When done, remove potatoes from oven at once.
4. With fork, prick each potato to let out steam. Immediately cut 1½-inch cross in top of each. Then, holding each potato with clean towel, press from bottom until snowy interior bursts through; break up lightly with fork. Top with salt, butter, and paprika.
5. Serve at once (to avoid sogginess), passing a tray of toppings.

BROCCOLI SUNBURST

2 10-ounce packages frozen broccoli spears	⅓ cup mayonnaise
2 tablespoons butter or margarine	2 tablespoons grated Parmesan or sharp-
1 tablespoon lemon juice	Cheddar cheese
2 egg whites	Paprika
	Lemon wedges

About 20 minutes before serving:
1. Cook 2 packages of broccoli together as package labels direct, using double the amount of boiling salted water that 1 package calls for.
2. Meanwhile, melt butter in small saucepan; remove from heat; stir in lemon juice. Set aside.
3. Preheat broiler 10 minutes, or as manufacturer directs. Place rack on low shelf if range has a separate broiler, or on middle shelf it it's an oven broiler.
4. In medium bowl beat egg whites until stiff. With rubber spatula, gently fold in mayonnaise.
5. Drain cooked broccoli spears and arrange in sunburst design (stem ends to center) in 10-inch glass pie plate (a 9-inch pie plate will do if stems are trimmed to fit). Pour butter-lemon juice mixture over flower end of broccoli. Spoon egg-white mixture in round heap over center where stems meet. Top with grated cheese, then lightly sprinkle with paprika.
6. Place under broiler for 2 to 3 minutes, or until cheese has melted and egg-white mixture is puffy and light-golden-brown.
7. Serve immediately, garnished with lemon wedges. Makes 6 to 8 servings.

GINGER CRÈME PIE

1 package regular butter-scotch-pudding-and-pie-filling mix	1 cup heavy cream
	½ teaspoon vanilla extract
1 teaspoon ground ginger	½ cup coarsely-chopped walnuts
½ package piecrust mix	6 to 8 walnut halves
1 envelope unflavored gelatin	Slivers of crystallized ginger

Early on day:
1. Prepare pudding mix as package label directs, using only 1½ cups milk and adding ground ginger. Place a piece of wax paper directly on surface of pudding; refrigerate.
2. From piecrust mix prepare 8-inch pie shell having a high fluted edge. Bake as package label directs; remove from oven and cool.
3. When both butterscotch pudding and pie shell are cool, sprinkle gelatin over ¼ cup cold water in measuring cup; set cup in pan of hot water and stir to dissolve gelatin, then remove from heat.
4. Beat cream with vanilla until thick; then beat in gelatin until mixture is just stiff.
5. Beat butterscotch pudding until smooth; fold in chopped walnuts and whipped cream. Turn mixture into pie shell; top with walnut halves and crystallized ginger. Refrigerate until serving time. Makes 8 servings.

DELECTABLE DUET
*Ham and Fig Fritters**
*Orange-and-Green Salad**
Bread Sticks
Lemon Meringue Pie
Coffee

HAM AND FIG FRITTERS

1 tablespoon salad oil	2 ¾-pound ready-to-eat ham slices, ⅜ inch thick
1 cup peeled small white onions	
⅓ cup water	1 teaspoon prepared mustard
½ teaspoon salt	⅓ cup maple syrup
⅛ teaspoon pepper	1 tablespoon cider
Fig Fritters, page 40	1 tablespoon lemon juice

About 45 minutes before serving:
1. To salad oil, in skillet, add onions; sauté until lightly browned. Add water, salt, and pepper. Cook,

Three-Layer Beef and Vegetable Loaf

Veal Cutlets Magnifico

Ham and Fig Fritters

tightly covered, about 15 minutes, or until tender, adding a tablespoon more water, if needed.

2. Meanwhile, make Fig Fritters; keep warm.

3. Remove onions to heated serving platter; keep warm. Pour drippings from skillet; then, in skillet brown one of ham slices on both sides; remove to platter.

4. In same skillet, brown second ham slice, then remove to platter. Rearrange ham, onions, and fritters *as pictured on page 39.*

5. Into ham drippings stir mustard; add maple syrup, cider, and lemon juice. Heat; spoon over ham. Makes 4 servings.

FIG FRITTERS

Salad oil	½ teaspoon double-acting
1 egg	baking powder
2 tablespoons milk	⅛ teaspoon cinnamon
½ cup sifted regular all-	⅛ teaspoon mace
purpose flour	¼ teaspoon nutmeg
½ teaspoon salt	12 packaged pulled dried
	figs with stems

1. In deep saucepan or electric skillet heat ½ inch salad oil to 365°F. on deep-fat-frying thermometer.

2. Meanwhile, make this batter: In medium bowl, beat egg with milk and 1 teaspoon salad oil; into it sift flour with salt, baking powder, cinnamon, mace, and nutmeg; stir until blended.

3. Now, holding each fig by stem, dip bottom of it into batter to ½ inch depth. Then set in saucepan of oil, and fry, a few at a time, until golden. Drain on crushed paper towels. Makes 12 fritters.

ORANGE-AND-GREEN SALAD

2 9-ounce packages frozen	⅓ cup Italian dressing
whole green beans	¼ teaspoon dried savory
2 medium carrots	

At least 1 hour ahead:

1. Cook beans as package labels direct; drain, then refrigerate until chilled.

2. Meanwhile, with vegetable parer, shave pared carrots lengthwise into ribbons; wrap in foil; refrigerate.

Just before serving:
Toss green beans and carrots with dressing and savory. Makes 4 or 5 servings.

REGAL FARE
A Sparerib Crown*
Buffet-Style Vegetable Platter*
Tossed Salad with French Dressing
Fruit Sherbet   Coconut Cookies
Coffee

A SPARERIB CROWN

2 pounds prunes	½ cup packaged cracker
2 small strips (racks)	meal
fresh spareribs	1 tablespoon prepared
4 large cooking apples,	mustard
pared, diced	1 teaspoon salt
3 large stalks celery,	1 tablespoon bottled sauce
diced	for gravy
4 small onions, diced	2 tablespoons water
2 lemons	1 16-ounce jar spiced
½ cup butter or margarine,	whole crab apples
melted	Water cress

Day before:
Cook prunes as package label directs; cool, then pit and coarsely snip. Refrigerate.

About 3 hours and 30 minutes before serving:

1. Stand strips of spareribs upright and shape into hollow crown; fasten together with string or skewers. Place on heavy-duty foil in shallow roasting pan.

2. In large bowl combine prunes, apples, celery, onions, grated peel and juice from lemons, melted butter, cracker meal, mustard, and salt.

3. Start heating oven to 350°F.

4. Fill spareribs with prune mixture, packing it, then mounding top. Cover with foil.

5. Roast 2 hours; then remove foil and brush sides of crown with combined bottled sauce for gravy and water. Roast 1 hour longer.

6. Remove crown to serving platter by inserting 2 wide spatulas under foil. Tuck foil under crown so it does not show. Garnish with crab apples and water cress *as pictured on page 42.* Makes 8 to 10 servings.

BUFFET-STYLE VEGETABLE PLATTER

Long straight carrots	Dash garlic salt
1 16-ounce can whole beets	1 pound zucchini,
⅓ cup commercial sour	diagonally sliced
cream	1 teaspoon salt
1 tablespoon prepared	1 10-ounce package frozen
horse-radish	Fordhook limas

Early on day:

1. With vegetable parer, shave lengthwise strips from

pared carrots. Curl each strip up tightly, then place them on ice cubes, tucking them in tightly; refrigerate.

2. Drain beets; with tip of apple corer make a small hole, part way down, in each beet; refrigerate.

3. Blend sour cream with horse-radish and garlic salt; refrigerate.

About 25 minutes before serving:

1. Cook zucchini in water to cover with salt until just fork-tender; drain; season to taste.

2. Also cook limas as package label directs; season.

3. Meanwhile, fill beets with horse-radish mixture. On platter, arrange beets, carrot curls, zucchini, and limas *as pictured on page 42.* Makes 6 servings.

TIME-HONORED FAVORITES
Baked Pork Chops   Scalloped Potatoes
Colorful Slaw*
Double-Boiler Boston Brown Bread*
Orange Custards*   Coffee

COLORFUL SLAW

4 cups finely-shredded cabbage	1 cup shredded Cheddar cheese
½ cup minced onion	½ cup mayonnaise
1 cup canned pineapple chunks	2 tablespoons lemon juice
⅓ cup coarsely-chopped pimento	1 teaspoon salt
½ cup sliced stuffed olives	¼ teaspoon pepper
	½ cup heavy cream

About 1 hour and 30 minutes before serving:
In large bowl toss together, cabbage, onion, drained pineapple chunks, pimento, olives, and cheese; refrigerate, covered.

About 10 minutes before serving:

1. In large bowl place mayonnaise; stir in lemon juice, salt, and pepper; mix until smooth.

2. In medium bowl, with mixer at medium speed, or hand beater, beat cream just until it peaks. Gently fold whipped cream into mayonnaise mixture.

3. Pour mayonnaise mixture over cabbage mixture, then toss well with fork. Makes 8 servings.

DOUBLE-BOILER BOSTON BROWN BREAD

1 cup raisins	1¼ teaspoons baking soda
1 tablespoon regular all-purpose flour	¾ teaspoon salt
¾ cup rye flour	½ cup plus 1 tablespoon molasses
¾ cup yellow corn meal	1½ cups buttermilk
1½ cups sifted regular all-purpose flour	

Early on day, or day before:

1. Grease well inside of top of 1½-quart glass double

boiler. Cut a circle of foil 1 inch wider than double boiler cover, then lightly grease one side of it.

2. Place raisins in bowl; add boiling water to cover; let stand 5 minutes. Drain well; dry slightly on paper towels; transfer to dry bowl and mix lightly with 1 tablespoon all-purpose flour.

3. In medium bowl mix rye flour, corn meal, 1½ cups all-purpose flour, baking soda, and salt. Thoroughly blend molasses with buttermilk, then stir into flour mixture until well mixed; if lumpy, beat gently with hand beater just until smooth. Fold in raisins.

4. Pour batter into top of double boiler. Place foil, greased side down, on top, then cover tightly. Set in double-boiler bottom which contains enough boiling water to come up to at least 3 inches around top part. Cook, over low heat, 4 hours; keep water boiling constantly, and do not uncover. Replenish water from time to time, to keep at original level.

5. At end of 4 hours, remove cover and test center of bread with cake tester; it should come out clean. If top seems a bit wet, that's all right—it will firm up when cool. Remove from boiling water; loosen edges of bread with spatula, then turn out immediately on greased plate. Or, if drier bread is desired, place on cookie sheet and dry out in 300°F. oven for 30 minutes. Then cool and refrigerate, wrapped in foil.

At serving time:
Serve hot or cold, in slices with butter, cream cheese, or cottage cheese. To reheat, bake foil-wrapped slices in 325°F. oven 15 minutes, then serve. Makes 1 loaf.

ORANGE CUSTARDS

4 eggs	1 teaspoon vanilla extract
¼ cup granulated sugar	Nutmeg or flaked coconut
¼ teaspoon salt	Orange Sauce, page 43
2½ cups milk*	

Early on day:

1. Start heating oven to 300°F. Grease 6 custard cups.

2. Into large bowl break eggs; with mixer at medium speed, or hand beater, beat until fluffy. Add sugar and salt; beat until thick and lemon-colored. Add milk and vanilla; beat again until thoroughly combined.

3. Pour mixture through fine strainer into custard cups, filling each to ½ inch from top; sprinkle with nutmeg or coconut. Set cups in shallow baking pan; place on oven rack. Fill pan with hot water to ¾ inch from top of cups.

4. Bake about 1 hour. Near end of baking time, insert silver knife into center of custards; it should come out clean. Remove at once from oven; cool on wire rack. Refrigerate. Make Orange Sauce.

At serving time:
Run spatula around inside of each custard, then unmold in a ring on serving plate. Spoon some of sauce over

Buffet Style Vegetable Platter

A Sparerib Crown

Boer Chicken Pi

Chicken, Danish Styl

each; place rest of sauce in small pitcher set in center of orange "flower," made as directed below. Makes 6 servings.

*For a richer custard use part cream.

ORANGE SAUCE: In small saucepan combine ¼ cup granulated sugar with 1 teaspoon cornstarch. Slowly stir in 1 cup orange juice and 1 tablespoon grated orange peel. Cook over medium heat, stirring constantly, until thickened; then stir in ¼ teaspoon almond extract; let cool.

To make orange "flower:" Cut skin of 1 large orange into 8 "petals," from top almost down to bottom. Peel skin from orange, petal by petal, but do not separate petals as base. Lift out all orange sections, leaving orange "flower."

SOMETHING SCANDINAVIAN
Chicken, Danish Style*
Tossed Boston-Lettuce Bowl
Crisp Cheese Crackers
Pineapple Sherbet   Coffee

CHICKEN, DANISH STYLE

1 5½-pound roasting chicken	1 9-ounce package frozen whole green beans
Water	½ cup regular all-purpose flour
Salt	
15 peppercorns	1½ tablespoons prepared horse-radish
Few celery leaves	
2 bay leaves	2 tablespoons prepared mustard
Few parsley sprigs	
6 medium potatoes, pared	2 egg yolks, beaten
4 medium carrots, cut into 1½-inch crosswise slices	5 thin dill-pickle slices
	2 tablespoons snipped parsley
1 pound small white onions	

About 1 hour and 45 minutes before serving:
1. Place chicken in large kettle or Dutch oven with 1½ quarts water, 1 tablespoon salt, peppercorns, celery leaves, bay leaves, and parsley sprigs; bring to boil; simmer, covered, 50 minutes. Add potatoes; bring to boil, then simmer, covered, 20 minutes, or until chicken and potatoes are tender.
2. Meanwhile, simmer carrots with onions in 2 cups water with 2 teaspoons salt, covered, 15 to 20 minutes; add frozen green beans and cook 5 minutes, covered, or until vegetables are tender-crisp; drain and keep warm.
3. With 2 large spatulas, lift chicken from kettle and place in center of large heated platter; arrange potatoes along one side of chicken; keep warm.
4. Strain chicken broth, reserving 3 cups. In medium saucepan mix flour with ½ cup cold water, beating until smooth; add reserved chicken broth, ½ teaspoon

salt, horse-radish, and mustard; bring to boil, stirring, then simmer 5 minutes. Add part of this sauce to beaten egg yolks, stirring constantly; stir into rest of sauce in saucepan and heat just to boil. Spoon part of sauce over chicken, covering it; pass rest in gravy boat.
5. Cut one of cooked carrot pieces into thin slices; place each one on a pickle slice, then use to garnish breast of chicken, securing each with a toothpick.
6. Place rest of carrots, onions, and beans along other side of chicken *as pictured opposite*; sprinkle parsley over potatoes, then serve at once, removing toothpicks. Makes about 6 servings.

SOUTH-AFRICAN TRADITION
Boer Chicken Pie*
Tossed Mixed Green Salad
Orange Muffins* with Sweet Butter
Fresh Blueberries with Lemon Sherbet
Iced Coffee

BOER CHICKEN PIE

2 3-pound stewing chickens, quartered	4 hard-cooked eggs, sliced
Salt	¼ cup butter or margarine
1 teaspoon whole allspice	¼ cup regular all-purpose flour
1 teaspoon peppercorns	⅓ cup sherry
3 bay leaves	2 tablespoons lemon juice
3 medium carrots, halved	¼ teaspoon mace
3 celery stalks, halved	¼ teaspoon pepper
3 medium onions, quartered	2 egg yolks
About 10 parsley sprigs	1 package piecrust mix
¼ pound cooked ham, sliced, then quartered	1 egg, beaten

Day before, or early on day:
1. In large kettle bring chickens to boil in 1 quart water with 1 tablespoon salt, allspice, peppercorns, and bay leaves. Add carrots, celery, onions, and parsley; simmer, covered, 30 minutes, or until vegetables are tender-crisp.
2. Remove vegetables and chickens from kettle; strain broth. Slice carrots and celery diagonally, ½ inch thick. Carefully cut chicken meat from bones in chunks, removing skin. In 12-by-8-by-2-inch baking dish, arrange chicken, vegetables, ham, and hard-cooked eggs.
3. In saucepan melt butter; stir in flour, then gradually add 2 cups chicken broth, sherry, lemon juice, mace, 1 teaspoon salt, and pepper. Cook, stirring, until thickened.
4. Beat egg yolks, then slowly stir into sauce; heat, stirring, until thickened, *but do not boil*. Pour over chicken.
5. Prepare piecrust mix as package label directs, then roll out to 14-by-10-inch rectangle. Fold in half crosswise; unfold, as top crust, over chicken. Turn overhang

HOT CHICKEN "SOUPREME"

6 10½-ounce cans con- densed cream-of-chicken soup, undiluted	4½ cups water Grated lemon peel or nutmeg
3 cups commercial sour cream	

1. Into soup stir soup cream and water until smooth. Heat, *don't boil*, stirring occasionally.
2. Serve in mugs, sprinkled with lemon peel or nutmeg. Makes 12 servings.

BUFFET BEANS EN CASSEROLE

6 tablespoons melted butter or margarine	1½ teaspoons chili powder
3 cups sliced onions	¾ teaspoon salt
6 cloves garlic, crushed	1 tablespoon prepared mustard
9 cups drained canned kidney beans	12 frankfurters, sliced diagonally, ½ inch thick
2¼ cups red wine	

About 45 minutes before serving:
1. In butter in 4-quart Dutch oven, sauté onions and garlic until golden. Add beans, wine, chili powder, salt, mustard, and frankfurters.
2. Heat, covered, over low heat, stirring occasionally, 15 to 20 minutes, or until hot. (Or, if more convenient, bake covered, at 400°F. 1 hour and 15 minutes, or until hot, then bake, uncovered, 5 minutes.) Makes 12 to 16 servings.

PERFECT BUFFET FARE
*Cold Sliced Chicken and Ham
Shrimp and Rice à la Peak of Perfection*
Lettuce Wedges   Green Onions   Stuffed Olives
Fruit Tarts   Finger-Cakes
Iced Tea*

SHRIMP AND RICE À LA PEAK OF PERFECTION

4½ quarts cooked rice	2 envelopes unflavored gelatin
1 quart finely-sliced Pascal celery	1 cup water
½ cup chopped green pepper	3 cups mayonnaise
2 cups shredded raw carrots	48 large unshelled shrimp, cooked (about 3¼ pounds)
¼ cup chopped pimento	½ bunch parsley
¼ cup chopped stuffed olives	Bottled sweet-spicy French dressing

Day before:
1. Have on hand 10-, 7-, and 4-inch tiered aluminum cake-pan set. Oil pans well.

2. Cook rice as package label directs, omitting butter. Then fluff up rice and set aside to cool.
3. In each of 2 large bowls combine half of celery, green pepper, carrots, pimento, stuffed olives and rice.
4. Over low heat, dissolve gelatin in water. Then gradually stir and blend into mayonnaise. Pour half of mayonnaise mixture over rice mixture in each bowl; blend well.
5. Pack rice mixture into oiled pans. Cover; refrigerate. Shell and devein shrimp. Fill small slit down back of each with finely-snipped parsley. Refrigerate.
Just before serving, next day:
1. Unmold 10-inch pan by running spatula around inside of pan, then inverting it on serving dish. Repeat with other pans, inverting, tier by tier, on largest one.
2. Over top of each tier, arrange shrimp, with one in center top. Garnish with parsley sprigs. Serve with bowl of dressing for dipping. Makes 24 servings.

CALIFORNIA TREASURE
Lobster Thermidor with Curried Rice* and Chutney
Buttered Broccoli with Lemon Slices
Hearts-of-Palm Salad*   Giant Popovers
Sherbet-Filled Orange Shells with Coconut
Hot Coffee*

LOBSTER THERMIDOR

12 8-ounce frozen rock- lobster tails	2 teaspoons salt
Boiling water	6 tablespoons sherry
¾ cup butter or margarine	4 cups light cream
½ cup regular all-purpose flour	Curried Rice, page 60
¼ teaspoon nutmeg	½ cup grated process Cheddar cheese
Paprika	Chutney

Early on day:
1. Boil unthawed rock-lobster tails in salted water to cover (1 teaspoon salt per 1 quart water), allowing 3 minutes longer than ounce weight of largest tail—for example, 11 minutes for 8-ounce tails. Drain; cool.
2. With scissors, carefully cut away thin underside membrane, then, with fingers, pull out meat. Snip lobster meat into chunks. Wash, then reserve shells. Refrigerate all until needed.
About 1 hour before serving:
1. In large double boiler melt butter; stir in flour, nutmeg, generous dash paprika, salt, and sherry. Slowly add cream, stirring constantly; then add lobster chunks. Cook over hot water, stirring occasionally, until just thickened.
2. Meanwhile, start Curried Rice.
3. Preheat broiler 10 minutes, or as manufacturer directs.
4. Fill reserved lobster shells with hot lobster mixture.

under; press firmly to edge of dish; make scalloped edge.

6.   In center of top crust, with knife, cut out rectangle 7 by 3 inches. At each corner of rectangle make a ½-inch diagonal slit, then turn its piecrust edges up to form a scalloped edge *as pictured on page 42.* With remaining dough and small cookie cutter, cut out small designs; arrange over top of piecrust; then refrigerate.

About 45 minutes before serving:

1.   Start heating oven to 425°F.

2.   Brush pie with beaten egg. Bake 30 minutes, or until golden and hot. Makes 8 servings.

ORANGE MUFFINS

2 cups sifted regular all- purpose flour	1 egg
3 teaspoons double-acting baking powder	¾ cup milk
	¼ cup orange juice
½ teaspoon salt	¼ cup grated orange peel
¼ cup granulated sugar	¼ cup salad oil or melted shortening

1.   Start heating oven to 425°F. Grease 14 2½-inch muffin-pan cups well.

2.   Sift flour with baking powder, salt, and sugar.

3.   Beat egg until frothy; stir in milk, orange juice, orange peel, and salad oil; mix well. Make small well in flour mixture; pour in milk mixture, all at once. Stir quickly and lightly—*don't beat—until just mixed, but still lumpy.*

4.   Quickly fill muffin cups two-thirds full; wipe off spills of batter. (If batter does not fill all cups, fill empty ones with water to keep grease from burning.)

5.   Bake 25 minutes, or until cake tester, inserted in center of muffin, comes out clean.

6.   To serve, run spatula around each muffin to loosen; then tip slightly in pans; keep warm. Makes about 14.

A TASTE OF THE ORIENT
Ducklings with Ginger Sauce* on Orange Rice*
Chinese Cabbage*
Sesame Melba Toast
Crunchy Peanut Pie*   *Coffee*

DUCKLINGS WITH GINGER SAUCE

1 tablespoon instant minced onion	Orange Rice, below
	Water cress
1 teaspoon salt	2 tablespoons slivered crystallized ginger
½ teaspoon pepper	
2 4- to 5-pound ready-to- cook ducklings	Ginger Sauce, below

About 3 hours and 45 minutes before serving:

1.   Start heating oven to 325°F.

2.   Combine instant minced onion, salt, and pepper; sprinkle over ducklings inside and out. With poultry pin or toothpick fasten neck skin to back on each bird.

Place birds, breast side up, on rack in shallow, open roasting pan.

3.   Roast 2¾ to 3 hours, or until thick portion of legs feels soft when pressed, and legs can be moved easily.

4.   Meanwhile, make Orange Rice and Ginger Sauce.

5.   To serve, remove poultry pins. Spoon Orange Rice onto large heated platter. Arrange ducklings on top, with water cress in body openings. Sprinkle ducklings with crystallized ginger, then spoon on some of Ginger Sauce. Pass rest of sauce. In serving, cut ducklings in quarters. Makes 8 servings.

ORANGE RICE: About 1 hour before serving, cook favorite rice as package label directs—enough to make 6 to 8 cups, cooked; keep hot. In large skillet or Dutch oven, in ¼ cup butter or margarine, sauté 2 cups thinly-sliced (on an angle) celery until just tender-crisp. Add rice, 1 teaspoon salt, and speck pepper; toss well. Then add 3 oranges, sectioned, and toss just enough to mix them in. Keep warm until served.

GINGER SAUCE: In saucepan combine ⅓ cup light- or dark-brown sugar, packed, ¼ cup granulated sugar, and 1 tablespoon cornstarch. Add 1 cup orange juice, ¼ teaspoon salt, and ¼ teaspoon ground ginger. Stir, over low heat, until sugars dissolve. Simmer until transparent and thickened—about 3 minutes. Then add 1 tablespoon slivered crystallized ginger. Keep warm until serving time. Makes about 1½ cups.

CHINESE CABBAGE

¼ cup butter or margarine	½ teaspoon salt
1 medium head Chinese cabbage	⅛ teaspoon pepper
	6 sprigs water cress
¼ cup boiling water	

About 15 minutes before serving:

1.   In large skillet melt butter. Meanwhile, cut cabbage into crosswise slices, 1¼ inches wide. Wash gently, dry, then set in skillet, cut-side down. Add boiling water; sprinkle with salt and pepper.

2.   Cook cabbage, covered, over medium heat, 8 to 10 minutes, or until fork-tender. Tuck water cress between cabbage rounds.

3.   Serve, spooning some of juices from skillet over cabbage and cress. Makes 8 servings.

CRUNCHY PEANUT PIE

1 unbaked 9-inch pie shell	1 cup white corn syrup
4 eggs	2 tablespoons melted butter or margarine
¼ teaspoon salt	
1 cup dark corn syrup	1 cup salted peanuts

Day before:

1.   Make 9-inch pie shell with fluted edge; then, with 4-tined fork, flatten each point on edge. Refrigerate.

2.   Start heating oven to 350°F.

3. With hand beater, or mixer at medium speed, beat together eggs, salt, and dark and white corn syrups until well blended; add melted butter; then blend.
4. Spread salted peanuts over bottom of unbaked pie shell; pour egg mixture over them.
5. Bake pie 45 minutes; cool, then refrigerate until next day, to thoroughly chill before serving. Makes 10 servings.

EASY ELEGANCE
Chicken Sauterne* on Fluffy Rice
Stuffed, Crystallized Apples*
Hot Crescent Rolls
Raspberry-Cherry Parfaits   Coffee

CHICKEN SAUTERNE

3 whole chicken breasts	½ teaspoon celery salt
1½ teaspoons salt	½ teaspoon paprika
1 package frozen green	½ teaspoon orégano
peas with onions	½ teaspoon Worcestershire
1 pound small mushrooms	¼ teaspoon Tabasco
Butter or margarine	½ cup sauterne wine
3 tablespoons regular all-	1 cup light cream
purpose flour	Hot, fluffy rice
1 tablespoon instant minced	
onion	

About 1 hour before serving:
1. Simmer chicken breasts in water to cover, with 1 teaspoon salt, covered, until tender—about 30 minutes. Then remove skin and bones, leaving chicken in large pieces; reserve 1 cup chicken broth.
2. Meanwhile, cook peas with onions as package label directs. Stem mushrooms. In 2 tablespoons butter, in skillet, sauté mushroom caps until golden-brown; remove.
3. In same skillet melt 3 tablespoons butter; stir in flour, instant minced onion, ½ teaspoon salt, celery salt, paprika, orégano, Worcestershire, and Tabasco. Stir in chicken broth and wine. Stir, over low heat, until thickened. Cool slightly; stir in cream, mushrooms, peas, and chicken; reheat (do not boil).
4. Serve on hot fluffy rice. Makes 8 servings.

STUFFED, CRYSTALLIZED APPLES

3½ cups water	1 3-ounce package cream
3½ cups granulated sugar	cheese
2 teaspoons lemon juice	¼ cup chopped pecans
8 small Winesap or	3 tablespoons prepared
Delicious apples	horse-radish
½ teaspoon red food color	Water cress

Two days before:
1. In Dutch oven boil water, sugar, and lemon juice 30 minutes.

2. Meanwhile, pare and core apples. Add food color to syrup; lower apples into it; cook moderately fast so syrup bubbles up over apples 15 minutes.
3. Turn; cook apples until transparent (this may take 35 minutes); cover; remove from heat; let stand 30 minutes.
4. Spoon syrup over apples. Refrigerate, uncovered.
Just before serving:
Lift apples to platter; fill with cream cheese mixed with pecans and horse-radish; tuck water cress in each. Makes 8.

HARVEST DINNER
Hens-in-the-Pot
Crusty Pecan Squash*
Tossed Raw Vegetable Salad   Corn Muffins
Meringue-Fruit Medley*
Coffee

HENS-IN-THE-POT

4 1-pound frozen Rock	1 tablespoon Worcester-
Cornish hens	shire
Butter or margarine	2 tablespoons lemon juice
1 teaspoon salt	1 cup red wine
¼ teaspoon pepper	8 small white onions
1 teaspoon thyme	8 small mushrooms
1 tablespoon regular all-	Fresh parsley and dill
purpose flour	

Day before:
Start thawing Cornish hens in refrigerator; reserve giblets for later use.
About 1 hour and 15 minutes before serving:
1. In 3 tablespoons melted butter, in large Dutch oven, sauté Cornish hens. When golden on all sides, sprinkle with salt, pepper, and thyme. Into butter around hens stir flour, Worcestershire, lemon juice, and wine. Simmer, covered, 40 to 50 minutes.
2. Meanwhile, in 3 tablespoons butter, in medium skillet, sauté onions until golden; add to Cornish hens. In same skillet, sauté mushrooms on all sides; add to

ens. Cook, covered, until hens and vegetables are tender.

3. At serving time, snip a sprig or two of parsley and dill over hens. Transfer them to serving platter, or serve directly from Dutch oven. Makes 4 servings.

CRUSTY PECAN SQUASH

2 12-ounce packages frozen squash, thawed	1 teaspoon salt
⅓ cup melted butter or margarine	½ teaspoon pepper
	½ teaspoon nutmeg
⅓ cup undiluted evaporated milk	½ cup coarsely-broken pecans
2 tablespoons brown sugar	2 tablespoons corn syrup

About 45 minutes before serving:
1. Start heating oven to 400°F.
2. In large bowl combine squash, melted butter, evaporated milk, brown sugar, salt, pepper, and nutmeg. Turn into greased 1½-quart casserole.
3. In small bowl combine pecans with white or dark corn syrup; sprinkle over squash.
4. Bake about 30 minutes, or until squash mixture is heated through. Makes 6 servings.

MERINGUE-FRUIT MEDLEY

4 egg whites, at room temperature	2 oranges, sectioned
1 cup granulated sugar	2 small bananas, sliced, dipped in orange juice
2 teaspoons vanilla extract	8 pitted, cooked prunes
20 unblanched almond halves	½ cup seedless green grapes
1 cup commercial sour cream	1 lemon slice, halved

Day before, or early on day:
1. Start heating oven to 200°F. Cover cookie sheet with brown paper; draw circle in center of paper by inverting a 9-inch pie plate on it and tracing around it.
2. In large bowl, with mixer at high speed, beat egg whites until soft peaks form. Now gradually add sugar, then vanilla, beating until stiff, glossy peaks form.
3. With spatula, spread meringue ¼ inch thick on paper circle. Then drop heaping teaspoons of meringue around circumference of circle, to form outer rim of shell. Smooth inside and outside of this rim with spatula until it stands about 1¾ inches high.
4. Now, going from inner edge of rim to opposite side, and using index finger and small knife or spatula as guides, spoon on remaining meringue in 4 crisscross strips, ½ inch wide, across bottom of shell, forming 8 equal wedge-shaped sections. Next, with tip of knife, swirl meringue at center of shell into peak; then press almond halves, cut side down, and slantwise, around side of shell.

5. Bake 2 hours, or until slightly golden and completely dry. Remove from oven; cool thoroughly before removing paper. (If meringue shell sticks to paper, moisten back of paper; let stand 5 minutes, then carefully remove.)

Just before serving:
Over bottom of each section of meringue spread layer of sour cream. Now fill first section with oranges, second with bananas, third with prunes, and fourth with grapes. Repeat in same order. Then insert half a lemon slice in outer edge of each prune section. In serving, cut into 8 wedge-shaped servings.

PERFECTION A LA PERINO
Peeled Grape Supreme*
Lobster Soufflé with Lobster Sauce*
Braised Endive
Cucumber Sandwiches on Thin Rye
Raspberry Sherbet topped with Crème de Cacao
Petit Fours   Coffee

PEELED GRAPE SUPREME

3 tablespoons lemon juice	¼ teaspoon salt
⅓ cup olive oil	Speck pepper
1 teaspoon liquid honey	1 pound seedless grapes, peeled
Dash dry mustard	

Day before:
Combine lemon juice, olive oil, honey, mustard, salt, and pepper; refrigerate.
At serving time:
Divide peeled grapes between 8 coupettes or sherbet glasses; spoon on dressing. Makes 8 servings.

LOBSTER SOUFFLÉ WITH LOBSTER SAUCE

3 small live Maine lobsters	¼ teaspoon pepper
3 quarts boiling salted water	1 cup regular all-purpose flour
1 cup butter or margarine	2 cups milk
Lobster Sauce, page 48	⅓ cup grated Parmesan cheese
7 eggs	
1¼ teaspoons salt	

Day before, or early on day:
1. Plunge lobsters, head first, into boiling salted water; cover; boil 10 minutes; drain.
2. To prepare lobster-butter, cut off lobster heads (about 2½ inches from front end), mash heads with potato masher in saucepan. Add butter; simmer slowly (don't boil) about 2 minutes; then strain butter into bowl (save heads).
3. Remove lobster meat from claws and tail (save shells). Slice tail meat thinly; refrigerate it and lobster-butter.

Baked Fish Feast

Curried Halibut Steaks

Stuffed Fillets of Sole

4. Make Lobster Sauce; refrigerate.

About 1 hour and 30 minutes before serving:

1. Start heating oven to 350°F. Butter, then flour, 2½-quart soufflé dish.

2. Separate eggs, placing whites in large bowl, yolks in small. Then measure ½ cup plus 2 tablespoons of lobster-butter (now solidified); heat in medium sauce-pan. Stir in salt, pepper, flour, then milk. Cook over low heat, stirring, until mixture is thick and leaves sides of pan—about 5 minutes. Remove from heat; vigorously stir in sliced lobster tails and grated cheese.

3. Beat egg whites until stiff but not dry. Beat egg yolks until light and fluffy; fold into lobster mixture; then fold lobster mixture into egg whites. Turn into soufflé dish.

4. Bake 1 hour and 5 minutes. Serve immediately, with Lobster Sauce, heated. Makes 8 servings.

LOBSTER SAUCE: In large saucepan mash claw and tail shells; add reserved lobster heads, 1½ cups water, ½ small onion, cut up, 1 stalk celery, cut up, 2 sprigs parsley, ⅛ teaspoon dried thyme, and 1¼ teaspoons salt; cook about 20 minutes. Strain off broth; add claw meat and speck pepper. Refrigerate.

WELCOME!
Stuffed Fillets of Sole*
Baked Tomato Halves
Green Salad with Blue-Cheese Dressing
Crusty French Bread
Coconut Cake
Coffee

STUFFED FILLETS OF SOLE

2 tablespoons butter or margarine	½ teaspoon salt
2 4½-ounce cans shrimp, drained	Pepper
	Paprika
1 3- or 4-ounce can mush-rooms, chopped, drained	2 10½-ounce cans con-densed cream-of-mush-room soup, undiluted
1 large onion, minced	¼ cup water
2 tablespoons snipped parsley	⅓ cup sherry
8 sole fillets (about 3 pounds)	½ cup grated process Cheddar cheese

Early on day:

1. In hot butter, in skillet, sauté shrimp, mushrooms, onion, and parsley until onion is soft.

2. Sprinkle both sides of each fish fillet with salt, pepper, and paprika. Onto one end of each fillet, spoon some of onion mixture; then roll up fillet, securing with toothpick. Place fillets in attractive 12-by-8-by-2-inch baking dish.

3. In medium bowl combine soup, water, and sherry; pour over fillets; sprinkle with grated cheese; refrigerate.

About 40 minutes before serving:

1. Start heating oven to 400°F.

2. Sprinkle fillets and sauce with paprika. Bake fillets 30 minutes, or until easily flaked with fork, *but still moist.* Serve right from baking dish *as pictured on page 47.* Makes 4 to 6 servings.

THE LOOK OF LUXE
Salade Nicoise*
Curried Halibut Steaks*
Hot Rolls
Company Crème Brûlée*
Coffee

SALADE NICOISE

1 9-ounce package frozen whole green beans	½ teaspoon prepared mustard
1 2-ounce can anchovy fillets	1 small clove garlic, crushed
Milk	½ cup olive oil
3 medium tomatoes	3 tablespoons lemon juice
1½ teaspoons salt	½ cup thinly-sliced cucumber
½ head iceberg lettuce	4 hard-cooked eggs, quartered lengthwise
¼ teaspoon freshly-ground black pepper	Pitted ripe olives
1 teaspoon granulated sugar	

About 20 minutes before serving:

1. Cook green beans 1 minute less than label directs, then refrigerate at once. Soak anchovy fillets in a little milk to reduce saltiness.

2. Skin tomatoes by letting them stand in boiling water 8 to 10 minutes and then peeling; then cut into ¼-inch slices; sprinkle with 1 teaspoon salt. Tear lettuce into bite-size pieces; wash; drain.

3. Combine pepper, sugar, mustard, garlic, and ½ teaspoon salt in small bowl; then add olive oil and lemon juice; mix well.

4. Place lettuce in salad bowl; over it sprinkle a few teaspoons of dressing; then layer cucumber slices,

quartered eggs, tomato slices, green beans, and more dressing until all are used, ending with beans.

5. Over beans lay anchovy fillets lattice-wise; then decorate with ripe olives. Serve as appetizer course. Makes 6 to 8 servings.

CURRIED HALIBUT STEAKS

2 halibut steaks, 1½ pounds each	¼ cup snipped parsley
Salt	¾ teaspoon curry powder
1½ cups cooked rice	5 tablespoons butter or margarine, melted
1½ cups fresh bread cubes	About 3 bacon slices (optional)
½ cup finely-chopped celery	Lemon wedges
½ cup minced onion	Parsley sprigs

About 1 hour and 15 minutes before serving:
1. Start heating oven to 350°F.
2. Sprinkle steaks with 1½ teaspoons salt.
3. In large bowl, with fork, toss together well rice, bread cubes, celery, onion, 2 tablespoons snipped parsley, curry powder, 1 teaspoon salt, and 2 tablespoons melted butter.
3. In well-greased 13-by-9-by-2-inch baking dish place one steak. Spread rice mixture over steak; place second steak on top; secure with toothpicks.
4. Combine 3 tablespoons melted butter with 2 tablespoons snipped parsley; pour over steaks.
5. Bake 40 to 50 minutes, or until fish flakes easily when tested with fork.
6. Cook bacon slices until crisp; keep warm.
7. When halibut steaks are done, remove from oven and serve, right from baking dish, garnished with diagonal pieces of crisp bacon, lemon wedges, and parsley sprigs *as pictured on page 47.* Makes 8 servings.

COMPANY CRÈME BRÛLÉE

1 package regular vanilla-pudding-and-pie-filling mix	¼ cup slivered toasted almonds
1½ cups milk	Orange sections
1½ cups heavy cream	Banana chunks, dipped in lemon juice
½ cup light-brown sugar, packed	Thin slices fresh pineapple
	Tiny bunchlets grapes

Day before:
Make vanilla pudding as package label directs, substituting 1½ cups milk and 1½ cups heavy cream for 2 cups milk called for. Pour into 1½-quart shallow baking dish; lay piece of foil directly on surface of pudding; refrigerate.
About 1 or 2 hours before serving:
1. Preheat broiler (rack removed) 10 minutes, or as manufacturer directs.
2. Meanwhile, sift brown sugar over top of pudding;

then sprinkle almonds in a ring, 1 inch in from edge. Set crème on broiler rack, 3 inches from heat.
3. Broil just until sugar melts, making a shiny carmel top. Refrigerate at once.
At serving time:
Set crème on large platter, with fruits arranged attractively around it. On each dessert plate, hostess places a serving of orange, banana, and pineapple with a bunchlet of grapes at side; then she spoons crème over fruits (except grapes). Or guests may help themselves. Makes 8 servings.

EAT HEARTY—STAY HANDSOME
Baked Fish Feast* with Hot, Fluffy Rice
Celery Sticks and Radishes
Hot Corn Bread
Fruit and Cheese Tray   Coffee

BAKED FISH FEAST

1 6-ounce can whole mushrooms	¼ teaspoon garlic powder
Butter or margarine	1 large broad cod or haddock fillet, about 2 to 2½ pounds
1 medium onion, minced	
½ green pepper, chopped	¼ cup grated Swiss cheese
1 celery stalk, chopped	
¼ cup snipped parsley	6 medium tomatoes, cut in ½-inch slices
Seasoned salt	
Salt	Few parsley sprigs
1 teaspoon dried basil leaves	6 lemon wedges

About 1 hour and 15 minutes before serving:
1. Reserve 6 whole mushrooms; slice rest (refrigerate mushroom liquid for later use).
2. In medium skillet, in 2 tablespoons butter, sauté onion until golden; then add green pepper, celery, sliced mushrooms, parsley, ½ teaspoon seasoned salt, ½ teaspoon salt, basil, and garlic powder. Sauté a few minutes; set aside.
3. Start heating oven to 400°F.
4. Sprinkle fish fillet with 1 teaspoon salt and 1 teaspoon seasoned salt. Place fillet along center of large oven-proof platter or 13-by-9-by-2-inch baking dish. Spread mushroom mixture along center of fillet, then fold fillet in half lengthwise, securing it with toothpicks. Over fillet sprinkle grated cheese, then dot with 2 tablespoons butter.
5. Bake 20 minutes; then remove from oven; arrange tomato slices along one side, place mushrooms here and there over tomatoes; sprinkle with 1 teaspoon salt. Bake 15 to 20 minutes longer, or until fish flakes easily with fork, *but is still moist.*
6. Before serving, remove toothpicks. Garnish fish with parsley sprigs and lemon wedges *as pictured on page 47.* Makes 6 servings.

Serving a crowd of 12 or more presents some problems not encountered when entertaining fewer guests. More than likely the service will be buffet-style, unless you have lots of space or care to hire a hall. § Plan your menu carefully—the more do-ahead dishes the better. Casseroles are particularly good for serving large numbers. And

When It's 12 or More

check china, silver, glasses, etc., to make sure you have plenty. You can mix china patterns, so don't worry if you have to use two or more. (These days no one frowns on paper plates, cups, and napkins—even disposable paper trays are acceptable in the best circles.) List the cooking utensils you will need. Plan to buy or borrow any extras to take care of large quantities of food. § Clear the decks. Temporarily put away items in the kitchen or pantry that might get in the way of efficient and convenient preparation and service. Make space in your refrigerator. Have on hand bowl covers, foil, plastic bags, etc., for wrapping and storing foods. § Enlist the help of a guest or two to lend a hand in the kitchen at serving time, and make arrangements for some clean-up assistance as well, so you don't get left with a mess. And above all, don't panic. With organization and planning, serving a crowd can and should be fun. Starred recipes (*) in menus appear below them.

Big Event Buffet

BIG EVENT BUFFET
Salad Bouquet of Fresh Fruit*
Cold Curried Chicken Salad with
Curry Accompaniments*
Spicy Layered Coleslaw* with Golden Dressing*
Assorted Hot Breads   Iced Tea

SALAD BOUQUET OF FRESH FRUIT

4 1-inch slices watermelon	Cracked ice
2 quarters large honeydew	24 lettuce leaves
2 quarters large cantaloupe	¼ cup snipped glacéed
2 pounds green grapes	cherries
1 pound purple grapes	¼ cup slivered almonds
2 unpeeled oranges	

About 2 hours before serving:
Cut watermelon into pie-shaped wedges. Halve each quarter of honeydew and cantaloupe crosswise. Snip washed grapes into small bunches. Thinly slice oranges. Refrigerate.

At serving time:
Fill 2 large, deep oblong servers with cracked ice. Cover with lettuce leaves. Arrange fruits on lettuce, sprinkling cherries and almonds over orange *as pictured on page 50.* Guests help themselves—no dressing needed.

FOR 48: Double all ingredients; proceed as directed, using large deep servers or punch bowl.

COLD CURRIED CHICKEN SALAD

8 quarts boiling water	2 tablespoons curry powder
2 tablespoons salt	2 tablespoons salt
2 16-ounce packages	1 teaspoon pepper
regular white rice	1 cup milk
12 to 14 cups cooked	2 cups thin green-pepper
chicken or turkey,	strips
in large chunks	4 cups celery, cut on
2 cups raw cauliflower,	angle
in ¼-inch slices	2 cups thinly-sliced red
2 8-ounce bottles creamy-	onions
style French dressing	2 heads romaine
2 cups mayonnaise or	Curry Accompaniments,
cooked salad dressing	below

Day before:
1 To boiling water add 2 tablespoons salt, then rice; cook, covered, over low heat, until rice feels tender between fingers. Drain, if necessary, then place in roasting pan. When cool, refrigerate, covered.
2. Cut cooked chicken or turkey into chunks; refrigerate, covered.
Early on day:
1. Toss rice with cauliflower and French dressing; cover and refrigerate at least 2 hours.
2. In large pan combine mayonnaise, curry powder, 2 tablespoons salt, and pepper; slowly stir in milk; add

chicken; toss. Refrigerate, covered, at least 2 hours.
Just before serving:
In large bowl or pan combine rice mixture with chicken mixture; then add green pepper-strips, celery, and onions. Turn out onto platter lined with romaine leaves. Serve with Curry Accompaniments *as pictured on page 50.* Makes 24 servings.

CURRY ACCOMPANIMENTS: Flaked coconut, canned French-fried onion rings, salted peanuts, canned pineapple cubes, currant jelly, and tomato wedges. You may also add one or all of these: chutney, raisins, snipped parsley, crisp bacon bits, chopped hard-cooked eggs, sweet or sour pickles, sliced avocados, or grated orange peel.

SPICY LAYERED COLESLAW

4 small heads cabbage	4 Bermuda onions
(18 cups)	4 bunches radishes
6 large cucumbers	Golden Dressing, below
8 green peppers	

Day before, if desired:
1. Finely shred cabbage. With vegetable parer, pare cucumbers in lengthwise strips. Cut crosswise into thin slices. Refrigerate all, wrapped.
2. Wash, seed, then cut green peppers into ¼-inch crosswise slices. Slice peeled onions ⅛ to ¼ inch thick. Wash and slice radishes very thinly. Refrigerate all, wrapped.
3. Prepare Golden Dressing; refrigerate.
At serving time:
1. In 16- or 18-quart glass punch bowl arrange about one-fourth cabbage; on top arrange cucumbers in layer. Cover with another fourth of cabbage; then green peppers in a layer. Top with half remaining cabbage, then onion rings, then rest of cabbage, heaped high in center. Around top outer edge of coleslaw arrange radish slices, row upon row, *as pictured on page 50.*
2. Just before serving, toss slaw with some of Golden Dressing. Serve rest of dressing in carafe or pitcher. Makes 24 servings.

FOR 48: Double ingredients above, using 16- or 18-quart punch bowl and refilling as needed.

GOLDEN DRESSING

6 cups mayonnaise or	2 tablespoons granulated
cooked salad dressing	sugar
3 tablespoons salt	¾ cup vinegar
1½ teaspoons pepper	¾ cup milk
1½ teaspoons paprika	¼ cup prepared mustard
	12 egg yolks

Several days ahead, if desired:
Combine all ingredients in order listed; blend well. Refrigerate, covered. Makes about 9 cups.

FOR 48: Use 3 quarts mayonnaise, 6 tablespoons salt, 1 tablespoon pepper, 1 tablespoon paprika, ¼ cup sugar, 1½ cups vinegar, 1½ cups milk, ½ cup prepared mustard, and 24 egg yolks; proceed as directed. Makes about 5½ quarts.

COOL IDEA
Double Tomato-Aspic Rings* with
Tuna-Chinese Noodle Salad*
Marinated-Vegetable Mélange*
Hot-Deviled-Ham Rolls*
Finger Fruits   Almond-Topped Cookies
Espresso

DOUBLE TOMATO ASPIC RINGS

Canned tomato juice	5 envelopes unflavored
3 stalks celery	gelatin
2 small onions, sliced	½ cup vinegar
4 lemon slices	Lettuce or other greens
2 bay leaves	Tuna-Chinese Noodle Salad,
3 teaspoons salt	below
¼ teaspoon pepper	

Early on day:
1. In large saucepan combine 7½ cups tomato juice, celery, onions, lemon slices, bay leaves, salt, and pepper. Simmer, uncovered, 10 minutes; strain.
2. Meanwhile, sprinkle gelatin over 2 cups tomato juice and vinegar to soften; then add hot tomato mixture, stirring until gelatin is dissolved. Pour this mixture into 2 5-cup ring molds; refrigerate until firm.
About 30 minutes before serving:
On bed of lettuce, unmold tomato rings, side by side. Refrigerate until serving time, then fill center of each with Tuna-Chinese Noodle Salad *as pictured on page 54.* Makes 12 servings.

TUNA-CHINESE NOODLE SALAD

3 6½- or 7-ounce cans tuna	1 teaspoon salt
⅔ cup diced cucumber or	Speck pepper
sliced celery	¼ cup lemon juice
¼ cup chopped green	½ cup canned Chinese
pepper	noodles
¼ cup chopped pimento	2 8-ounce containers small-
¼ cup minced onion	curd cottage cheese

Early on day:
1. Drain tuna, reserving liquid.
2. In medium bowl combine tuna, cucumber, green pepper, pimento, onion, salt, and pepper. Refrigerate with tuna liquid.
About 15 minutes before serving:
1. Combine 2 tablespoons reserved tuna liquid with lemon juice. Pour over tuna mixture; then add Chinese noodles; toss well.

2. With knife, line center of each unmolded tomato ring with half of cottage cheese. Heap half of tuna mixture in each. Makes 12 servings.

MARINATED-VEGETABLE MÉLANGE

2 14¼-ounce cans chicken	2 10-ounce packages frozen
broth, undiluted	Fordhook limas, partially
2 bay leaves	thawed and broken into
Salt	chunks
Pepper	2 cups bias slices fresh
½ pound small white onions	asparagus, ½ inch
4 cups thin, diagonal	thick
carrot slices	¼ cup olive oil
2 9-ounce packages frozen	½ cup lemon juice
whole green beans,	½ teaspoon dry mustard
partially thawed and	½ teaspoon brown sugar
broken into chunks	1 clove garlic, minced
	Snipped parsley (optional)

Early on day:
1. In chicken broth, with bay leaves, 4 teaspoons salt, and ½ teaspoon pepper, in covered kettle, cook onions and carrots 5 minutes.
2. Now, on top of onions and carrots place beans, limas, then asparagus; sprinkle with 1 teaspoon salt. Cover; bring to boil; boil 8 to 10 minutes, or until vegetables are tender-crisp. Now drain, and refrigerate.
3. Combine olive oil, lemon juice, mustard, brown sugar, garlic, ½ teaspoon salt, and ¼ teaspoon pepper; refrigerate.
At serving time:
Strain dressing, if desired; then toss well with vegetables and parsley *as pictured on page 54.* Makes 12 servings.

HOT DEVILED-HAM ROLLS

12 finger rolls	1 teaspoon prepared
Soft butter or margarine	mustard
2 4½-ounce cans deviled	¼ teaspoon Worcestershire
ham	

Early on day, if desired:
1. Slit each finger roll in half, part way through. Spread with butter.
2. In small bowl combine deviled ham, mustard, and Worcestershire; blend well.
3. Spread each finger roll with some of deviled-ham

Lobster Gregor

"Thousand Layer" Cookie Torte

Cool Idea

mixture. Then arrange on cookie sheet; cover with foil; refrigerate.

About 20 minutes before serving:
1. Start heating oven to 350°F.
2. Bake wrapped rolls 15 to 20 minutes. Unwrap; serve at once *as pictured opposite*. Makes 12 servings.

CONTINENTAL CUISINE
*Lobster Gregor**
Salad Verte   Green and Ripe Olives
Bread Sticks   Cheese Cubes
*"Thousand-Layer" Cookie Torte**   *Tea*

LOBSTER GREGOR

Herb Puff Paste, page 18
Boiling water
2 medium onions
½ cup vinegar
1 teaspoon salt
Parsley
6 1-pound Maine lobsters
    or 6 frozen rock-lobster
    tails, unthawed
4 cups strained lobster
    broth

½ cup butter or margarine
½ cup regular all-purpose
    flour
2 9-ounce packages frozen
    artichoke hearts,
    thawed, quartered
½ cup sherry
2 teaspoons salt
¼ teaspoon pepper
2 tablespoons lemon juice
1 egg white

One to three days before serving:
Make up Herb Puff Paste; refrigerate, wrapped.
About 2 hours before serving:
1. To 4 quarts boiling water, in large kettle, add onions, vinegar, 1 teaspoon salt, and a few sprigs parsley. Add lobsters; cook 13 minutes, then remove lobsters and drain, reserving 4 cups lobster broth.
2. In large double boiler, or 3-quart saucepan, over direct heat, melt butter. Slowly stir in flour, then cook, stirring constantly, until smooth (do not let this *roux* take on any color). Gradually stir in lobster broth, then continue stirring until boiling. Now set double-boiler over boiling water and cook, 1 hour, stirring occasionally.
3. Start heating oven to 425°F.
4. Remove lobster meat from shells, being sure to remove claw meat without breaking it. Cut rest into chunks. Wrap claws in foil and refrigerate.
5. In medium bowl, place artichokes; pour on boiling water to cover; let stand 10 minutes; drain. Add to sauce in double boiler, with sherry, salt, pepper, lemon juice, and lobster chunks. Heat, over boiling water, 20 to 30 minutes, or until hot.
6. Meanwhile, on floured board, roll out Herb Puff Paste to a rectangle 16 by 12 inches. Using fluted pastry wheel, cut into strips 1 inch wide. On large cookie sheet, draw outline of serving dish about 15 by 9 by 1 inch. On outline lay pastry strips, lattice fashion, until it is filled in. Brush with slightly beaten egg white.

7. Bake 15 to 20 minutes, or until golden.
Just before serving:
1. Arrange lobster mixture in serving dish. Carefully loosen puff paste from cookie sheet and slide it onto top of lobster; if necessary, with scissors, trim it to just fit edges of dish.
2. Over ends of pastry, lay garnish of parsley sprigs. Stand chilled lobster claws upright between lattice strips *as pictured opposite*. Makes 12 servings.

"THOUSAND-LAYER" COOKIE TORTE

1 cup butter or margarine,
    softened
1½ cups granulated sugar
3 eggs
½ cup milk
2 teaspoons vanilla
    extract
5 cups sifted regular all-
    purpose flour

½ teaspoon salt
3 teaspoons double-acting
    baking powder
Prune or Apricot Filling,
    page 56
Lemon Frosting, page 56
1 cup heavy cream or 1
    package dessert topping
    mix

Several days before:
1. In large bowl, with mixer at medium speed, beat butter with sugar until light and fluffy. Beat in eggs, one at a time, then milk and vanilla, mixing well.
2. Sift flour with salt and baking powder; add to butter mixture, one cup at a time, blending well after each addition. Cover; refrigerate overnight, or longer, if desired.
3. Using 9-inch layer-cake pan as a guide, cut 14 9-inch circles from wax paper.
4. Prepare Prune or Apricot Filling; refrigerate.
Day before:
1. Start heating oven to 375°F.
2. Remove enough dough from refrigerator to shape, with floured hands, into a 2-inch ball. On one of wax paper circles, with floured, stockinet-covered rolling pin, roll out dough to edges of circle (it will be very thin). Trim, if necessary, then transfer to ungreased cookie sheet.
3. Repeat, using a second cookie sheet; then bake on upper and lower racks, in same oven, about 12 minutes, or until lightly browned. While still on wax-paper circles, remove from cookie sheets to wire racks to cool. Repeat until all dough is used, making 14 circles and keeping unused dough in refrigerator.
4. When all layers are cool, gently stack them and cover with wax paper until needed.
5. Prepare Lemon Frosting; cover; refrigerate.
About 1 hour and 30 minutes before serving:
1. Peel wax paper from one cookie layer; place on cake plate. Spread with ½ cup filling. Repeat, peeling paper from each of 14 layers before it is stacked. If cookie layer should break, it can still be used.
2. Spread top cookie with Lemon Frosting; then grate

1 to 2 teaspoons lemon peel over entire top of frosting *as pictured on page 54.*

3. Allow torte to stand, unrefrigerated, 1 hour, or longer, before serving, to allow filling to soften cookies.

4. Just before serving, with mixer at medium speed, whip cream until it holds soft peaks. Heap in small bowl; pass to top torte wedges. Makes 16 servings.

PRUNE FILLING: In saucepan cover 2½ pounds dried prunes with water; cook until prunes are very soft. Cool; drain; then pit prunes; put prunes through medium blade of food grinder. To ground prunes add 1½ cups granulated sugar, 1 tablespoon lemon juice, 2 to 3 teaspoons ground cardamom seeds, 1 teaspoon nutmeg, and ½ cup sherry; mix well. Beat 2 egg whites until stiff; fold about ⅓ cup prune mixture into them, then fold this into rest of prunes. Cover; refrigerate.

APRICOT FILLING: In saucepan, cover 2 pounds dried apricots with water; cook until apricots are very soft. Cool, drain, then put apricots through medium blade of food grinder. To ground apricots add 1½ cups granulated sugar, 1 teaspoon nutmeg, 2 to 3 teaspoons ground cardamon seeds, ½ cup sherry, and 1 tablespoon lemon juice; mix well. Cover; refrigerate.

LEMON FROSTING: In small bowl, with mixer at medium speed, beat 2 tablespoons butter or margarine with pinch salt and ⅓ cup sifted confectioners' sugar until light and fluffy. Add ⅔ cup sifted confectioners' sugar and 1 tablespoon lemon juice alternately; beat until smooth. Blend in a few drops yellow food color. Cover; refrigerate.

DUDE RANCH SUPPER
Bologna Barbecue*
Twenty-Four-Hour Bean Salad* or
Strawberry-Nut Salad*
Crisp Potato Chips   Iced Fresh Scallions
Apple Pie Wedges
Hot Coffee or Tea

BOLOGNA BARBECUE

1 whole Bologna (about 6 to 7 pounds)	1 cup red wine
2 cups chili sauce	1 or 2 loaves French bread
1 teaspoon whole dried rosemary	1 or 2 8-ounce packages Cheddar cheese slices
	Butter or margarine

About 1 hour and 30 minutes before serving:

1. Remove casing from Bologna; make 6 or 7 diagonal cuts, each about 4 inches long and 1 inch deep, across top of Bologna. Lay Bologna diagonally across 2 large cookie sheets, placed end to end.

2. Start heating oven to 350°F.

3. In saucepan combine chili sauce, rosemary, and wine; heat just to boiling. With pastry brush, brush top and sides of Bologna with sauce.

4. Bake 1 hour, or until metal skewer or cake tester, inserted through meat, feels warm, basting Bologna occasionally with sauce.

5. Meanwhile, cut bread into 1-inch slices; lay on cookie sheet or jelly-roll pan.

6. When Bologna is ready, place 2 slices of cheese, or 1 slice, folded in half, in each cut. Return to oven a minute or so. Then remove, with 2 large spatulas, to large wooden platter or board.

7. Toast bread under broiler until golden; butter.

8. Reheat rest of sauce; pour into serving boat. Cut a few slices Bologna; arrange on platter *as pictured opposite.* Makes 20 to 24 servings.

TWENTY-FOUR-HOUR BEAN SALAD

2 15½-ounce cans cut wax beans	1 cup salad oil
2 16-ounce cans French-style green beans	1 cup cider vinegar
2 17-ounce cans kidney beans	1½ cups granulated sugar*
2 cups thinly sliced onions	1 teaspoon salt
	½ teaspoon pepper
	2 heads curly chicory

Day before:

1. In large bowl combine wax beans, green beans, and kidney beans, drained, with onions.

2. In jar combine salad oil, vinegar, sugar, salt, and pepper; shake until well blended. Pour over beans; cover with foil, then refrigerate until served, tossing occasionally.

At serving time, next day:

Arrange chicory on 2 large platters. Drain dressing from bean mixture, then pile beans lightly on chicory. (Or arrange chicory on individual salad plates and onto each plate spoon about ½ cup drained beans.) Makes 24 servings.

*For less sweet salad, reduce sugar.

STRAWBERRY-NUT SALAD

4 packages strawberry-flavor gelatin	6 medium bananas, mashed
2 cups boiling water	2 cups coarsely-chopped walnuts
4 10-ounce packages frozen sliced strawberries, thawed	2 pints commercial sour cream
2 1-pound 4-ounce cans crushed pineapple	2 heads lettuce

Day before:

1. In large kettle combine gelatin with boiling water, stirring until gelatin is dissolved. Then fold in, all at once, strawberries with juice, drained pineapple, bananas, and walnuts.

2. Turn half of strawberry mixture into two 12-by-

Bologna Barbecue

8-by-2-inch serving dishes as first layer. Refrigerate until firm—about 1 hour and 30 minutes.

3. Evenly spread top of each dish with sour cream. Gently spoon on rest of strawberry mixture, dividing equally between serving dishes; refrigerate.

Just before serving, next day:

Cut each dish of strawberry salad into 12 squares. Heap lettuce in bowl nearby. Makes 24 servings.

SUMMERY LUNCHEON
Cream-of-Tomato Soup (in mugs)
Potato Salad Supreme*
Brown 'n' Serve Rolls   Currant Jelly
Raw Relish Tray
Spiced Sliced Peaches   Brownies
Iced Coffee

POTATO SALAD SUPREME

6 cups cold, sliced cooked
   potatoes (about 2½
   pounds)
1 cup minced onions
½ cup finely-snipped
   parsley
½ cup finely-chopped
   celery
1½ teaspoons salt

¼ teaspoon pepper
2 envelopes unflavored
   gelatin
½ cup water
16 packaged cooked thin
   ham slices, each about
   7 by 4½ inches
1½ cups mayonnaise
Water cress

Day before:

1. In large bowl combine potatoes, onions, parsley, celery, salt, and pepper.

2. In measuring cup sprinkle gelatin on water; stir over hot water until dissolved.

3. Coarsely snip 8 ham slices; add to potato mixture along with mayonnaise mixture and gelatin; toss all together.

4. Line 10-by-5-by-3-inch loaf pan completely with foil, letting it extend about 3 inches above each edge. Now along 10-inch side of pan lay three overlapping ham slices, which extend across bottom of pan and up opposite side. Repeat on other side of pan, thus making double thickness of ham on bottom of pan. Then cover each end of pan with a ham slice. Have top of all slices even with top edges of pan.

5. Now pack potato mixture into ham-lined pan, then cover top of salad with overhanging foil. Refrigerate.

Just before serving:

Turn foil back from top of loaf and use it to lift salad from pan. Place chilled plate on top of salad; invert both; then peel off foil. Surround loaf with water cress. Serve in slices *as pictured.* Makes 12 servings.

SPUR-OF-THE-MOMENT BUFFET
Hot Chicken "Soupreme"* (in mugs)
Ham Loaf   Salami   Gouda Cheese
Buffet Beans en Casserole*
Long Thin French Bread
Sweet Pickles   Dill Pickles   Pickled Peaches
Tomato Wedges   Cucumber Fingers   Young Scallions
Rosy Radishes   Curry Mayonnaise
Brownie Bars à la Mode
Hot or Iced Coffee

Potato Salad Supreme

Sprinkle each with some of grated cheese and then lightly with paprika. Arrange filled shells in foil-lined jelly-roll pan.

5. Broil until just golden on top. Now arrange lobsters on large serving platter around center mound of Curried Rice *as pictured opposite*. Spoon chutney over rice. Makes 12 servings.

CURRIED RICE

Butter or margarine	2 tablespoons curry powder
4 cups uncooked regular or processed white rice	4 medium onions, minced
	2 quarts boiling water

About 45 minutes before serving:
1. Start heating oven to 400°F.
2. In ½ cup butter, in skillet, brown rice lightly; then place in shallow roasting pan. Stir in curry powder and minced onions. Pour on boiling water.
3. Bake, covered, 30 to 35 minutes, or until rice feels tender when pressed between fingers and all water is absorbed. Fluff up rice with 2-tined fork; keep warm until served. Makes 12 servings.

HEARTS-OF-PALM SALAD

3 heads iceberg lettuce, in bite-size pieces	¼ cup vinegar
2 avocados	¾ cup salad oil
3 14-ounce cans hearts-of-palm	1 teaspoon salt
	¼ teaspoon pepper

About 15 minutes before serving:
In a very large salad bowl combine lettuce, avocados, peeled and diced, and hearts-of-palm, drained, then sliced ¼ inch thick. In small jar combine vinegar, salad oil, salt, and pepper; shake well. Pour over salad; toss well. Makes about 15 servings.

COLLEGIANS HOME FOR SPRING VACATION
*Spring Ham Verde**
*Parmesan Potato Puffs**
*Dilled Cucumber and Green Bean Salad**
Corn Muffins
Chocolate Parfaits
Cola Beverage

SPRING HAM VERDE

3 12-ounce cans apple juice	1 cup finely-snipped fresh dill
4 envelopes unflavored gelatin	1 10- to 11-pound canned ham
2 cups finely-snipped parsley	Radish roses

Day before:
1. In saucepan heat 2 cups apple juice. Meanwhile, empty remaining apple juice into bowl; on it sprinkle

gelatin to soften. Stir in hot apple juice, then continue stirring until gelatin is dissolved. Stir in snipped parsley and dill; refrigerate until mixture starts to mound.
2. Meanwhile, remove ham from can as label directs, reserving bottom portion of can. Trim ham on all sides, top, and bottom, so it is about ½ inch smaller all around than the can. With sharp knife trim fat and gelatin from ham (grind trimmed pieces for later use in sandwiches or a soufflé).
3. Now carefully return ham to can. Pour around ham enough gelatin mixture to come up to top of ham, then pour rest of gelatin mixture over top of ham; smooth, if necessary, with a spatula Refrigerate 24 hours.
4. Make, then refrigerate radish roses.
Just before serving:
1. Run long spatula completely around gelatin layer to loosen it from can. Lay greased cookie sheet on top of can, then invert both; lift off can.
2. Place chilled serving platter on top of ham and invert ham and platter so gelatin layer is on top. Garnish with radish roses; serve sliced *as pictured opposite*. Makes 18 generous servings.

PARMESAN POTATO PUFFS

6 8-ounce packages frozen potato puffs	½ cup grated Parmesan cheese

About 40 minutes before serving:
1. Start heating oven to 350°F.
2. Spread frozen potato puffs in jelly-roll pan.
3. Bake puffs 30 minutes, stirring, with 2-tined fork, at end of 15 minutes of baking.
4. Then place puffs under broiler a few minutes to crisp and brown. Heap in layers with grated cheese, on hot serving plate. Makes 12 to 16 servings.

DILLED CUCUMBER AND GREEN BEAN SALAD

4 9-ounce packages frozen whole green beans	3 tablespoons powdered dill
4 cucumbers	1 tablespoon salt
2 cups commercial sour cream	½ teaspoon pepper
	2 tablespoons lemon juice

Early on day:
1. Cook beans as package labels direct; drain. Meanwhile, pare cucumbers and slice paper-thin. Then refrigerate beans and cucumbers at least 2 hours.
2. In small bowl combine sour cream, dill, salt, pepper, and lemon juice; refrigerate at least 2 hours.
Just before serving:
Toss beans and drained cucumber slices with sour-cream mixture until well coated; then arrange in 1 or 2 large serving dishes. Makes 16 servings.

Lobster Thermidor with Curried Rice

Spring Ham Verde

Luxury Low-Calorie Dinners

All of these dinners provide less than 500 calories, but who would ever guess! Flavor is the secret. Starred recipes (*) in menus appear below them.

Jellied Tomato Bouillon*
Flounder for a Few*
Salad Greens with Cottage Cheese
and Low-Calorie Dressing
Chilled Seedless Green Grapes
Coffee

JELLIED TOMATO BOUILLON

2 envelopes unflavored
   gelatin
Water
1 tablespoon lemon juice
4 beef-bouillon cubes or
   4 envelopes beef-broth
   mix

1 1-pint 2-ounce can
   tomato juice
½ teaspoon grated lemon
   peel
1 teaspoon Worcestershire
6 onion rings

Day before:
In medium saucepan, stir gelatin into ½ cup cold water; let stand 5 minutes to soften. Add lemon juice, bouillon cubes, tomato juice, 2 cups cold water, and lemon peel. Bring to boil, stirring occasionally; stir in Worcestershire. Refrigerate until set.
Just before serving:
Stir jellied soup, then ladle into cups to serve. Garnish with onion rings. Makes 6 servings. (*25 calories per serving*)

FLOUNDER FOR A FEW

4 carrots, cut into ½-
   inch slices
2 medium potatoes, cubed
2 medium onions, in thin
   rings
2 large celery stalks, cut
   into ½-inch slices
2 tablespoons finely-
   chopped pimento
¼ medium green pepper,
   finely chopped

1 pound frozen flounder
   fillets
1 to 1½ teaspoons salt
1 cup water
3 tablespoons regular all-
   purpose flour
¼ teaspoon poultry
   seasoning
1 can refrigerated biscuits

Day before:
1. Place prepared carrots, potatoes, onions, celery, pimento, and green pepper in large saucepan.

2. With sharp knife, cut frozen fillets into 1-inch cubes. Place over vegetables in saucepan; add salt and water. Cover; bring to boil, then simmer, gently, 15 to 20 minutes, or until vegetables are tender-crisp. Cool; then refrigerate.
About 45 minutes before serving:
1. Start heating oven to 425°F.
2. Heat vegetable-fish mixture to boil. Thoroughly drain broth from this stew, reserving broth; place stew in 2-quart casserole. Add water to broth, if necessary, to measure 1½ cups. In medium saucepan slowly add broth to flour and poultry seasoning, stirring constantly to make a smooth paste. Cook, stirring constantly, until thickened and smooth. Pour sauce over stew in casserole.
3. Place refrigerated biscuits on top of stew in an attractive pattern.
4. Bake 15 to 20 minutes, or until biscuits are dark golden-brown. Makes 5 servings. (*295 calories per serving*)

Appetizer Soup*
Broiled Lobster with Lemon Juice
Peas with Onion Rings
Celery Stalks filled with Seasoned Cottage Cheese
Strawberry Jelly Roll*
Hot Coffee

APPETIZER SOUP

6 cups water
4 beef-bouillon cubes
4 chicken-bouillon cubes
2 1-pound cans 3-ounce
   tomatoes
2 medium onions, chopped
1 cup thinly-sliced carrots

4 stalks celery, in ½-
   inch pieces
6 whole peppercorns
1 teaspoon sage
2 teaspoons salt
½ cup grated Parmesan
   cheese

1. In 4-quart saucepan, combine water, beef- and chicken-bouillon cubes, tomatoes, onions, carrots, celery, peppercorns, sage, and salt. Simmer, covered, 1 hour.
2. Serve sprinkled with Parmesan cheese. Makes 10 servings. (*60 calories per serving*)

STRAWBERRY JELLY ROLL

1 package angel-food cake
   mix
2 1-pound packages frozen
   whole strawberries,
   partially thawed
1 teaspoon unflavored
   gelatin

1 tablespoon cold water
Pinch salt
½ cup nonfat dry milk
   powder
½ teaspoon almond extract
1 tablespoon lemon juice
Red food color

1. Start heating oven to 375°F. Line bottom and sides of 15½-by-10½-by-1-inch jelly-roll pan with wax paper.
2. Prepare angel-food cake mix as package label directs; smoothly spread half of batter into prepared jelly-

roll pan. Pour remaining batter in unlined 9-by-5-by-3-inch loaf pan.

3. Bake both until golden—about 20 minutes for jelly-roll cake, 25 minutes for loaf cake.

4. Immediately after removing jelly-roll cake from oven turn out of pan onto lightly-sugared pastry cloth and peel off wax paper; let cool. To cool loaf cake, suspend pan upside down.*

5. While cakes are cooling, prepare filling: Refrigerate small bowl and beaters. Drain strawberries, reserving syrup; halve the large berries. Refrigerate 30 nice berries for decoration.

6. In small saucepan dissolve gelatin in cold water; add salt and ¼ cup reserved strawberry syrup; heat to melt gelatin; refrigerate until consistency of unbeaten egg white.

7. In chilled bowl mix nonfat dry milk, ½ cup reserved strawberry syrup, almond extract, and lemon juice; with mixer at high speed, beat until light and fluffy—about 10 minutes. Add partially-set gelatin mixture; beat 5 minutes more. Add drop of food color; mix well.

8. Set aside 1 cup filling for decoration; spread rest on jelly-roll cake, leaving ½-inch border on three sides and 2-inch border on one short side. Starting with 2-inch border, carefully roll up cake into jelly roll. Place on serving plate, seam down; refrigerate until serving time—not more than 1 hour.

9. To serve, slice with *very* sharp knife into 1-inch slices. Decorate each serving with a dab of filling, topped with a bud of three strawberries. Makes 10 servings. (*140 calories per serving*)

*Wrap and store angel-food loaf cake; slice and serve as "bread" for party sandwiches filled with preserves or melted semi-sweet chocolate.

*Chicken with Buttermilk Gravy**
Stewed Tomatoes
*Lettuce with Piquante Salad Dressing**
*Parfait Royale**   Coffee*

CHICKEN WITH BUTTERMILK GRAVY

1 tablespoon butter or margarine	1 teaspoon salt
1 small clove garlic	2 tablespoons chopped almonds (optional)
1 medium onion, chopped	2 cups buttermilk
4 chicken legs with thighs (about 1½ pounds)	2 tablespoons regular all-purpose flour
¼ teaspoon ground ginger	Paprika
1½ teaspoons curry powder	Dried parsley flakes

About 1 hour before serving:

1. In large, heavy skillet with tight-fitting cover, in butter, sauté garlic (stick a tooth pick in garlic so it can be retrieved) and onion until onion is lightly browned; remove garlic and discard.

2. Remove any obvious pockets of fat from chicken legs; sauté chicken legs until golden brown; remove from skillet.

3. Add ginger, curry powder, salt, and almonds to skillet; stir in 1 cup buttermilk; bring mixture to simmer, stirring constantly. Return chicken to skillet; simmer very gently, covered, 40 minutes, or until chicken is tender, but not dry, turning it occasionally.

4. Remove chicken to warm platter. Slowly mix remaining cup buttermilk into flour to form a paste, stirring. Slowly stir this paste into stock in skillet. Heat mixture almost to boil; stirring constantly. (Do not boil, or mixture—which is never absolutely smooth—will separate.)

5. To serve, pour some of gravy over each serving of chicken; sprinkle with paprika and garnish with parsley flakes; pass remaining gravy. Makes 4 servings. (*270 calories per serving*)

PIQUANTE SALAD DRESSING

½ cup water	¼ teaspoon paprika
1 cup tomato juice	¼ teaspoon onion salt
1 tablespoon cornstarch	½ teaspoon Worcestershire
2 tablespoons salad oil	
¼ cup vinegar	¼ teaspoon celery salt
1 teaspoon salt	Scant ⅛ teaspoon dry mustard
¼ teaspoon prepared horse-radish	2 dashes garlic salt

1. In small saucepan cook water, tomato juice, and cornstarch over low heat, stirring constantly, until clear and thickened.

2. Remove from heat; cool to lukewarm. Add remaining ingredients and beat, with hand beater or mixer, until smooth and well blended. Store, covered, in refrigerator. Shake well before using. Makes 1¾ cups. (*10 calories per tablespoon*)

PARFAIT ROYALE

1 1-pound can apple-raspberry sauce	2 cups skim milk or reliquified nonfat dry milk
1 1½-ounce package vanilla rennet powder	

1. Evenly divide one-half of sauce among 6 5-or-6-ounce parfait glasses or ¾-cup custard cups.

2. Prepare rennet custard as package label directs, using skim milk. Immediately divide rennet custard among parfait glasses; let stand in warm place until firm—about 10 minutes.

3. Spoon remaining sauce onto top of rennet custard; refrigerate until well chilled. Makes 6 servings. (*125 calories per serving*)

Index